INTERNET MARKETING FOR HOTELS

How to Use Search Engine Optimization,
Paid Search, Social Media and Other
Strategies to Promote Your Hotel
Or Other Lodging Property

This publication is designed to provide accurate and authoritative information in regard to the subject matter covered. It is sold with the understanding that the publisher is not engaged in rendering legal, accounting or other professional advice.

To learn more about the services offered by the author, visit www.WorkMedia.net or email Info@WorkMedia.net.

Table of Contents

Introduction

I've been involved in the field of Internet marketing in one capacity or another for 20 years and have run my own company, Work Media, for over a decade. I have had the good fortune to work with some of the biggest companies in the world. I have worked with law firms. I have worked with the makers of the finest barbecue sauce in Memphis. And I have spent many years doing online promotion for companies that own and operate various hotels. That experience is the basis for this book, which is about using the Internet to promote a hotel or other type of lodging business.

Internet marketing is not easy – especially in a competitive industry like hospitality. But it is extremely important. If you do not have a sound strategy for promoting your property, you are at a competitive disadvantage.

What you need is a system. And you need some time. I can't give you the time. But I can give you the system. Then you just have to be systematic about implementing it, either through your own efforts or by working with an experienced Internet marketing company.

I've tried to give you a good overall view of the different parts of an Internet marketing campaign, with just enough detail so you can dig in and get your hands dirty. I have left out certain technical details so as not to bog you down in too much information. It's not my intention to teach you how to build a website, but rather how to use a website to promote your property.

Let's roll.

Understanding the Basics

What Is Internet Marketing?

Internet marketing is using the Internet to promote your business, which could mean using Google to drive traffic to your website, promoting a Facebook business Page, sending a newsletter to an email list, running mobile phone ads, or any number of similar technologies.

Promoting your business online has a few advantages over traditional media marketing, like radio and print ads. These include:

- Online ads can be changed instantly. It can take days or weeks to change a traditional print, radio or TV ad.

- Ads can be automatically split-tested. Running two ads at once and comparing results can help you improve your ad performance.

- Budget can be changed any time. Need to run an ad for one day but only have $5? No problem. You can be on Google this afternoon.

- A growing advertising market. Everybody has a smart phone now. Everybody is using his or her phone to search for information. Businesses that take advantage of that will gain a competitive advantage.

- Personal connection. Internet marketing, and social media in particular, creates a communication channel that is much more personal than any kind of traditional media.

- Targeted marketing. Internet marketing can put your hotel in front of people looking for lodging in exactly your market.

There is a lot to like about Internet marketing.

The Components of an Internet Marketing Campaign

There are five main components to Internet marketing as I see it:

- Your website

- Search engine optimization (SEO)

- Paid search

- Social media

- Email

These are high level descriptions that have many sub-components. For example, "SEO" will include local SEO, which is the process of performing SEO specifically for a certain geographic market. A sound Internet marketing strategy makes use of all five of these components to some degree. The picture below illustrates how these components work together.

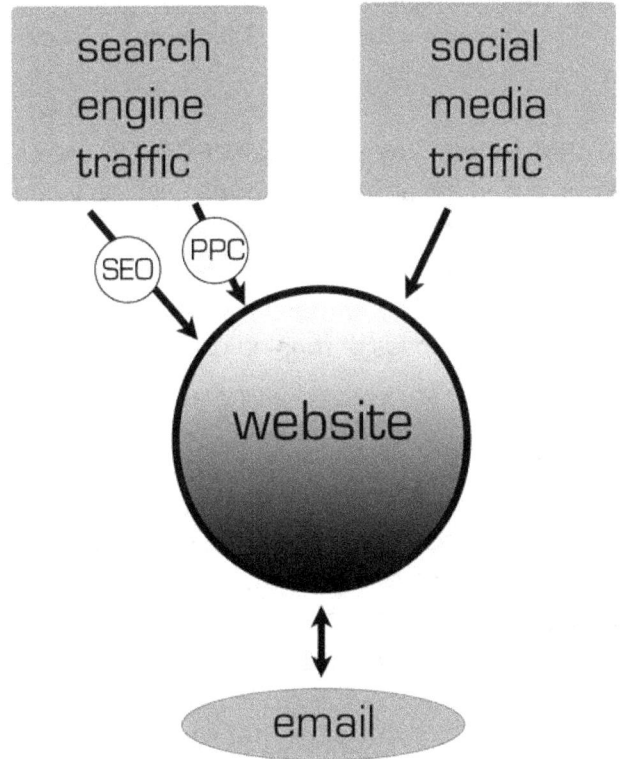

Your website. Your website is like your own little piece of Internet real estate. For a hotel, it is also where you will take reservations. It is also radically critical that your website be mobile friendly, which we will discuss later.

Search engine optimization (SEO). This is the process of optimizing a website so that it appears highly in organic (non-paid) search engine results for specific target keywords. So if you own a hotel in Gatlinburg, Tennessee, you would want your website to appear prominently in Google when someone searches for "Gatlinburg hotel." The things you do to make this happen are called SEO.

There is a category of SEO that deals specifically with optimizing a local business website to appear in local search results for its geographic market area. In this case, if a person is already in the

Gatlinburg area, you would like your hotel to appear when she searches "hotel" regardless if the word "Gatlinburg" is used in the search or not.

Paid search, also called "pay per click (PPC)". This is using one of numerous online advertising platforms such as Google AdWords or Bing Ads to drive traffic to your website. It generates a similar result as SEO, with the difference being that you actually pay a certain amount of money for each click. Included in this general category is the process of running graphical ads on third party (non-search) websites.

Social media. Facebook, Twitter and Google+ can all generate awareness for your business and drive traffic to your website. They also provide the opportunity to have one-on-one conversations with prospective customers. If you're going to use these to promote your business, you've got to be more strategic than just doing personal Facebook updates.

Email. I will make the wild assumption that you know what email is. In terms of Internet marketing, what we are talking about is building a list of email addresses of prospective or past customers to whom you send some kind of regular communication like a newsletter. For hotels in locations that are popular tourist destinations, this is an especially useful tool because you can keep your list updated on special events happening in the area. Tell them why they should come into town...and then sell them a hotel room!

When it comes to marketing and promoting your business on the Internet, you need to think 'multi-pronged." In other words, don't just use one strategy. Use a combination of different strategies to get your message out.

The great thing about Internet marketing is that many strategies don't require money. Only time. Now, time is the most valuable thing there is - but if you don't have money, then time is what you have to spend. And if you don't have enough of your own time, maybe you can spend somebody else's time. If you don't have somebody else's time...then at that point you might still have to spend some money to hire a company like mine. In that case, the information in this book will help you have a good understanding of the kind of help you need.

We'll start with a discussion of your website because that comes before all the other components. Then we will proceed to search engine optimization, which is the process that should start as soon as you have a website. Then we'll work our way through the other strategies.

But first, a little bit of marketing math...

Marketing Budgets

When you think in terms of "budget", you are generally assigning a fixed dollar amount to spend over a fixed amount of time - i.e., $1,000 per month.

A better way to think about marketing is in terms of cost per acquisition, or return on investment, as explained below.

Cost per Acquisition

This is how much it costs you to get a customer. If you spend $1,000 on marketing and get 10 customers, then your cost per acquisition is $100 ($1,000 divided by 10). Sometimes this is hard to figure out with a whole lot of certainty. But it is easier with Internet marketing than it is with other traditional forms of marketing.

Return on Investment

This is how much you generate in revenue above the cost of advertising, expressed as a percentage of your ad spend. So if for that $1,000 you spent above, you made $5,000, then your return on investment is 4x, or 400%, because you made $4 in earnings for $1 you spent ($5 revenue minus $1 spent on advertising).

In a later chapter, we are going to talk about conversions and conversion tracking, which are how you can make the above types of calculations.

Your Website

If you own a hotel and don't have a website…put this book down and go hire a website designer (or call me).

If your website is more than a few years old, it is probably time for a new one.

Internet marketing technology changes constantly. Google has recently begun placing a LOT more emphasis on mobile friendliness and load speed in ranking websites. Older websites usually don't pass the test.

Here are some factors that can play a critical role in the success of your site.

Domain Names

Your domain name is your friendly website address. If your hotel is a member of a large chain, then there may very well be corporate rules about what your domain can be. It may even have to be a sub-domain or folder of the corporate site. In this case, there is not really much you can do about it.

However, if you have the autonomy to use whatever domain name you want, then you have two basic options:

1. Use the name of your hotel as the domain; or

2. Use a keyword domain.

For example, if your hotel located in Pensacola, Florida is called Pensacola Lodge, then your domain name could be "pensacolalodge.com" or "Pensacola-florida-hotel.com".

Which approach is best? If you already have a lot invested in a particular brand name, then you are probably better of using that. However, if you are a newer property and there is keyword research data that shows there is a lot of traffic for the keyword version, then you should go with that. You could also register both and redirect one to the other. In that case, I would recommend redirecting the brand domain to the keyword domain, and then using the keyword domain as the target of your search engine marketing.

There are all kinds of different domain name extensions you can register these days, but I would still go with a .com if you can find one that works for you. My second choice would be a .net.

Website Hosting

There are places on the Internet that let you set up a website for free, such as WordPress.com. These types of sites do not require their own domain. But if you are serious about promoting your property online, then you're going to want to have your own domain name. That means you're going to have to have hosting.

Hosting is simply some space on a server (a certain type of computer connected to the Internet) where your website files can reside. The server "serves" your webpages to a person when he or she types in your web address in a program called a "browser."

You don't have to worry about the technical details. You just need to find a company you like and sign up. Companies that sell domain names are called "registrars." These days, most registrars also offer hosting. It might be easier to purchase your domain and hosting from the same company. The biggest and most well known domain registrar/hosting company is GoDaddy. But there are lots of other options.

There are different levels of hosting. The lowest and least reliable level is called "shared hosting." Shared hosting means there are multiple websites (sometimes many hundreds) on the same server. The advantage of shared hosting is that it is cheap. The disadvantage is that, with so many websites crammed onto the same server, shared hosted websites tend to be slower and less reliable.

A step up from standard shared hosting is something like a managed WordPress account. This is a type of shared hosting plan that is optimized for WordPress (which we will discuss later) and may be on a server with fewer other sites. It might cost a little more. Two options for managed WordPress hosting are GoDaddy and WPEngine. If those two, WPEngine is the better, more expensive option.

A big step up from that is a cloud hosting account. With cloud hosting, the website files are spread out among hundreds of different servers. It tends to be a lot more expensive. This is what I use for my business and the client sites I host. It is robust and very reliable.

Finally, you can even have your own dedicated server. This is by far the most expensive and complicated option. Unless you expect your website to have many thousands of visits every day, that is probably overkill.

Once you have a domain name and hosting, you have to create the pages that comprise your website. In their simplest form, Web pages consist of nothing more than text files coded with a sort-of scripting language called HTML ("HyperText Markup Language"). It would be possible for you to create your entire website using nothing more than a simple text editor. But these days, most websites are far more sophisticated than that, consisting of many different types of files that work together.

A better approach than doing everything manually is to build your website on a platform that creates all these files for you, so that all you have to do is log in and add your content. The most popular platform in the world for accomplishing this is called WordPress.

WordPress

If you are comfortable with technology, then you can certainly install WordPress yourself on a hosting account and begin using it. Or you can purchase pre-configured WordPress website hosting. Easiest of all is to pay an experienced website developer to do it for you.

A default WordPress installation is not all that attractive, but you make it more attractive and modern looking by installing what is called a "theme." A theme is a collection of files, templates and stylesheets that give the website a particular look. Taking it a step further, you can install any number of thousands of plugins that extend the functionality of WordPress and give you lots more flexibility with what you can do with it.

If you go with WordPress, there are companies now offering hosting just for that, and that might be a good idea to get the best performance. Here are the companies on the official list of WordPress hosts:

- Bluehost
- HostGator
- DreamHost
- InMotion Hosting
- SiteGround

WPEngine, mentioned earlier, is another hosting company that has become extremely popular for WordPress hosting.

My recommendation would be to either go with a higher level dedicated WordPress hosting account or a cloud hosting account. The speed of your website is very important, so don't skimp.

In your domain registrar account, you configure the domain so that requests for your website point to the right server. If you use separate domain and hosting companies, you will have to configure this manually. If you use the same company for both, it will probably be done automatically. Usually what you will configure is something called "name servers," which point the domain to the right server. Your hosting company will tell you what the name servers need to be.

Design Considerations

Some businesses can get away with boring, drab websites. Hotels? Not so much.

Your website needs to be beautiful. You need to have big, high resolution images of the exterior of your property, of your rooms, of your dining area, exercise room, pool...everything.

I would suggest that your site have at least the following content sections:

- Attractive home page
- Pages that describe each possible room configuration
- Blog
- Booking
- Conversion confirmation page

This should all be pretty obvious except for the last one. A conversion confirmation page is a page you can send the visitor to after booking a room. The purpose of that page is for conversion tracking. In other words, when somebody books a room, you would like to report the details of that transaction to an analytics account.

For example, if someone found your website by clicking on a paid ad in Google and then books a room, you would like to know the details. That is how you will know if your paid search ads or other marketing tactics are generating a positive return on your investment. We'll talk about conversion tracking in more detail later.

I'm not going to go into a whole lot more detail about what the site should "look" like. Look at websites for other top hotels and you will get some great ideas for your site. In fact, I highly recommend making a list of hotel websites you really like to show your website designer to give them something to go by.

So setting aesthetics aside, there are a number of other factors that must be taken into consideration, beginning with the speed of your site.

Website Load Speed

The faster a browser is able to load your website, the better. The faster your website is to Google, the better.

There are lots of different ways to increase how fast your website loads. I'm not going to get into a lot of them because some of it is pretty technical stuff. The first thing you need is high quality hosting, as discussed above.

Two other things that I will talk about here that you should know about are file caching and image compression.

File caching is a process whereby your web pages are stored somewhere in memory, either on the website server or on your own computer. The reason caching is useful for speeding up your website is that the server does not have to take the time to construct the web pages from all the different little pieces.

A web page is typically made up of all these different files that the server puts together to create the code that it sends to your computer or mobile device via the Internet. So if rather than having to go through that whole process, the server can just send you an HTML file that is all ready to go, that causes your web page to load quicker.

Image compression is the act of reducing the file size of the images on your website. The best way to do this is to reduce the file size yourself before you ever upload an image to the website. However, there are also plugins and such that will perform this as well.

There are a number of online tools you can use to test your website speed. Here are a few:

- https://developers.google.com/speed/pagespeed/insights/

- https://gtmetrix.com/

- http://www.speedtest.net/

It is a good idea to test your site with more than one tool and compare the results. If the results show that your website is too slow, then the problem could be any combination of the following issues:

- Poor performing website hosting.

- Too many plugins or other extra "stuff."

- Graphics that are too large.

- Not making use of any kind of caching.

Website load speed is even more important on mobile devices. More and more search traffic comes from mobile devices, and if Google detects that your site is too slow, it will not show it in mobile search results.

There are a million different reasons why your website might be slow to load. If you can't figure it out, you might want to hire some help to solve the problem.

Mobile Friendliness

Your website must be mobile friendly. This is not an option. It is a necessity.

If I have to scroll to the side to read your website on my phone, you have a problem.

If it takes forever for your website to load on my phone, you have a problem.

If I have to squint to read your website on my phone because the text is so small, you have a problem.

It could be more important for your website to be mobile friendly than it is to be optimized. Google is moving toward ranking sites based on mobile friendliness and load time above sites that just work well on a desktop computer. Look at your website on your phone. Make sure it is easy to read and navigate.

Here are some other rules for your website on mobile devices:

- Use large, easily readable fonts.

- No scrolling to the side.

- Easy navigation (often in the form of a dropdown rather than buttons).

There are two ways to deal with mobile. Your website can either send different web pages to mobile devices, or the website can use stylesheets to reformat itself for mobile (called "responsive" design). The responsive option is the best way to do it, and what Google prefers.

Here are a couple of examples to highlight what I am talking about as far as good design versus bad design.

Good Mobile Design

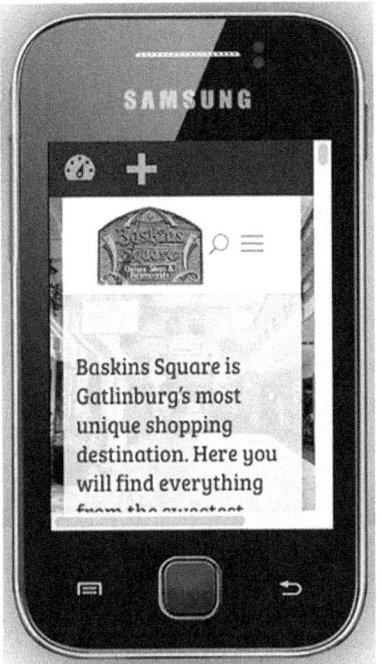

Notice that this website is very usable on this small phone screen. The logo fits into the top of the screen with a dropdown menu next to it for easy navigation. The text on the screen is nice and big and easy to read. There is no side-to-side scrolling.

Bad Mobile Design

Sorry Dickson County government, but your website looks crappy on this small screen. You can only see a tiny portion of the page and are going to have to scroll to the side several times to read all the way across. To see the different menu options, you will have to scroll sideways as well.

Virtual Tours

The better view you can give potential customers, the more likely they are to book rooms. A feature that has become very popular is virtual tours. These are immersive, 3-D experiences that allow website visitors to use their mouse or trackpad to virtually move around a room.

A virtual tour is created by taking a number of high resolution photos that are merged together into a type of file that is viewed in a plugin on your website. There are a number of companies that offer this service. A search of Google for "hotel virtual tours" will reveal a list of these providers. It is very likely there is a company in your market area that does it. When you hire a company to provide this service, it will send a photographer to take the required photos of whatever rooms are going to feature the virtual tour.

I could fill up a whole book about WordPress or website design in general, but that is not really our main point. If you need help setting up a website, find a qualified developer and your life will be a lot easier. Before starting the process, take the time to surf the Web and look at lots of other lodging websites. Make a note of the designs you like, the features you like...any kind of feature you would like for your website.

Copy

Let's talk about the words on your website – your copy. In general, more copy is better. For one thing, you will provide prospective customers with more information. On top of that, it helps with your search engine rankings. Tell the story of your property. Describe the different room configurations you offer. Talk about your amenities. And, of course, make it very easy to book a room.

Here are some rules to follow:

- Try to have at least 300 words in the copy on the main pages of your site. The more, the better.

- Use short sentences.

- Use shorter words whenever possible.

- Break your copy into short paragraphs.

The more words on your website, the better. But also keep in mind that reading on a screen is stressful on the eyes. Using short words, sentences and paragraphs makes reading easier.

Add new content to your website on a regular basis. There are a few good reasons to do this. For one thing, search engines like it. Google tends to favor websites that update often. The most typical way to update your website is through a blog.

Good subjects for blog posts for a hotel include:

- Upcoming events in the area.

- Reviews of local shops.

- Reviews of local dining.

- Holiday-related messages.

- News about what is going on at your property.

Content Updating

It is a very good idea to populate your website with new content on a regular basis. This serves several purposes:

- It encourages Google to return to your site to look for new content.

- It increases the number of pages on your site that could rank on a Google search results page.

- It creates material that you can feed into your Facebook and other social media accounts.

- It creates material you could use for an email newsletter.

The more often you can add new content to your website, the better. If you can add something every day, awesome. But one good article every 2 – 4 weeks is probably a good target to start with.

It is also a good idea to think in terms of keywords when coming up with article content. In other words, try to write articles about things that people are searching for online. Articles/blog posts are a great way to create keyword optimized content for your site, increasing the opportunities for generating search engine impressions for your website.

Shortly, we will discuss how to conduct keyword research. But for this moment, let's just say you have done some research and found that the phrase "Little Rock shopping" is a good traffic keyword for hotel in Little Rock, Arkansas. You could write a blog post titled "Best Little Rock Shopping Locations" that would have a reasonable chance at ranking on Google for that keyword.

The reason you would like for a page on your website to rank for a search phrase related to shopping is that some of those people searching for shopping destinations might also have need for a hotel. Maybe they're planning a shopping trip. Whatever. If it gets somebody to your website who is a possible customer, then that is a good thing.

If you want to be really slick about it, what you could do is pre-plan a series of articles mapped to particular keywords and schedule them out in advance.

In WordPress, you can set a blog post to appear at a later date. So you could go in and actually create the blog posts, set them to appear at certain dates, and then just leave them blank until you have a chance to get around to finishing the articles. If you do this, you need to make very sure that you actually do finish them before they get published. Otherwise, you will have a bunch of blank pages on your website.

You could also use a WordPress plugin to automatically update your social media accounts every time you do a new blog post.

I'm going to make the assumption that you will be using WordPress to manage your website. The next section relates to WordPress configuration. If you use another platform, these instructions may not apply.

WordPress Configuration

There are a few things you will need to configure in your WordPress settings in order to give your website a better chance at ranking in search engines.

Permalinks

Permalinks give your website URLs that are understandable by humans and search engines.

By default WordPress pages have URLs that consist of a ? followed by some variables. This is not good from a readability standpoint. It is a good idea for a human to be able to see the URL of the page and have a good understanding of what the page is about. Likewise, the URL is a place where you can place keywords for search engines.

To set up permalinks, go to Settings / Permalinks. I recommend setting it to "Post name," as shown below. What this means is that the title you give to a page or blog post will be used in the URL of the page.

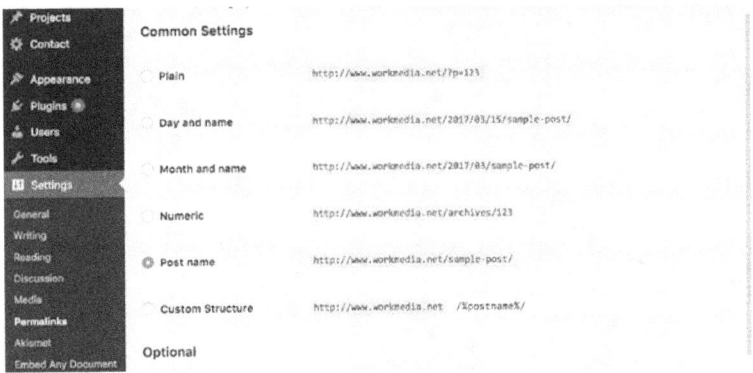

Another thing that I recommend you do is install an SEO plugin. There are a number of these, but one that I have used quite a bit is called Yoast SEO.

This discussion is based on the Yoast SEO plugin, but it should be a similar procedure for whatever particular plugin you use. On any given web page, there will be a place where you specify your target keyword for the page. Then the plugin will analyze the page to see if it is optimized adequately for your keyword.

As you tweak on the page to optimize it for your keyword, the plugin will give you feedback so you know if you have done what you need to do. For example, if your keyword is not contained in the page title or is not used enough in the copy, it will tell you that. Below is a screenshot to demonstrate what this looks like for a web page I optimized for the phrase "Kitec plumbing replacement."

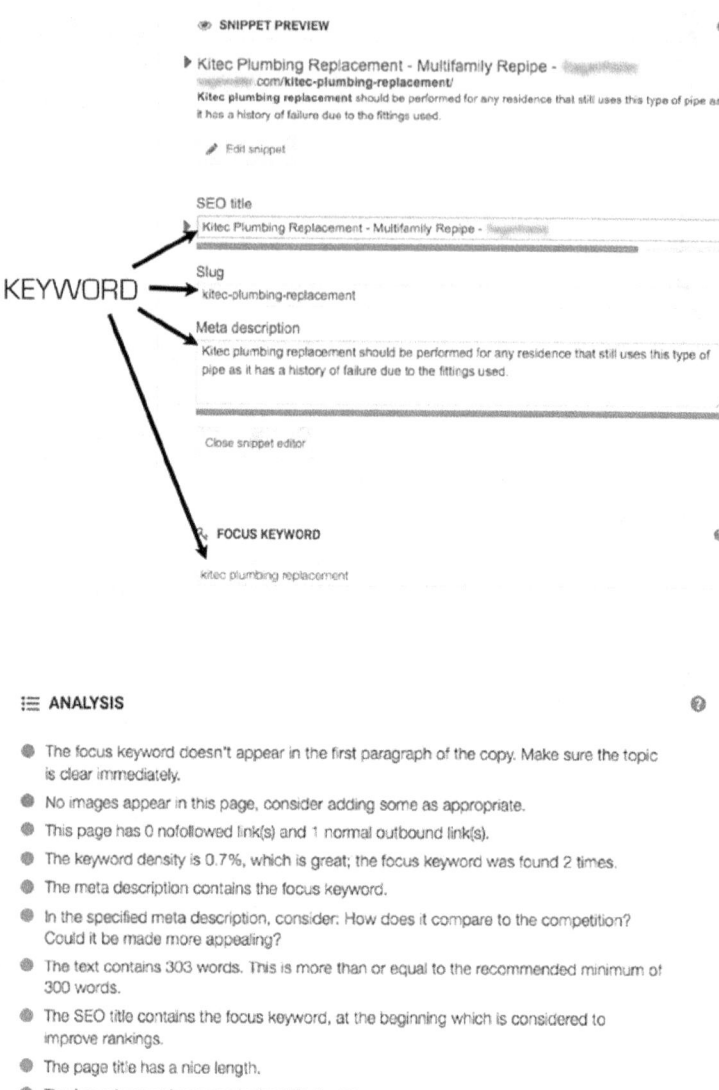

Basically, the plugin gives you your checklist of items you need to make sure you do on the page to optimize it for a particular keyword.

Shortly, we will get into the subject of on-page optimization, which will explain in more detail the items that the SEO plugin is checking.

Search Engine Optimization

Now let's talk about SEO, which is how you get Google or other search engines to show your website in search listings when someone in your area searches for whatever it is you are selling (without paying for it).

Keywords

Keywords are the words that people use to search the Web for a particular type of business or service. These words should be used strategically on your website to capture as much of that traffic as possible. A mistake that many business owners make is that they THINK they know what those words are, but they really don't.

Don't guess about what search terms someone might use to search for lodging in your area. Perform a process called keyword research to find out for sure what those words are. Google provides its own keyword research tool that will give you solid data to tell you what keywords you should be targeting.

How to Do Keyword Research

Go to https://adwords.google.com/KeywordPlanner

You will need a Google AdWords account. Google AdWords is Google's advertising platform to allow you to pay for clicks to your website. You don't have to actually spend any money in this case. You just need to create an account so that you can gain access to the Keyword Planner tool.

There are also third party (non-Google) tools that will allow you to do keyword research, but I have always liked relying on Google's own data. Plus, it's free (unless you choose to run ads).

Once you are in Google AdWords, click Tools / Keyword Planner on the menu at the very top of the page to get to the keyword research tool.

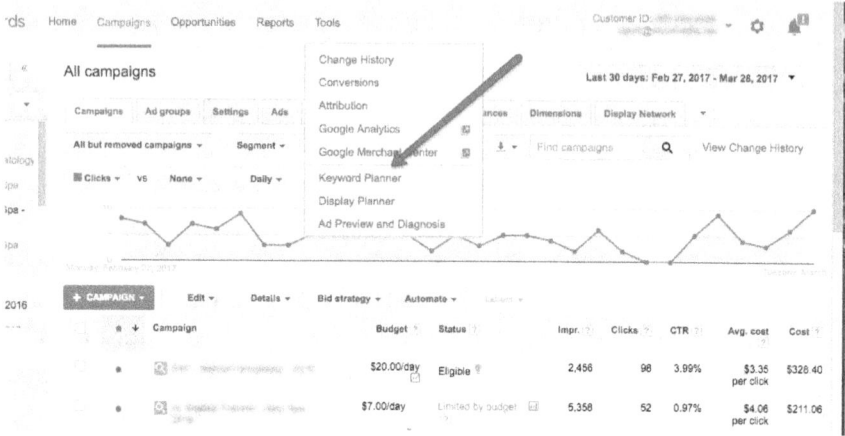

Click the box that says "Search for new keywords using a phrase, website or category." Then type in a few keywords related to your business.

Obviously you should target keywords related to lodging. "Hotel", "motel", "cabin", "lodge", etc., are all good starting keyword ideas. But it doesn't necessarily have to even be a lodging-related keyword. Think "outside the box" as the kids like to say.

If you recall the list of possible blog topic ideas above, that is a guide for your keyword searches. Look for keywords based around local dining, attractions, events, etc. Basically anything that brings people to town – that is a possible keyword.

Back to Google, there are also various options you can set such as running reports for a particular geographic area. If you are based in a small town, then you may not return much data by selecting that as your market. If you do want to view data specific to your location, click the pencil icon next to "All locations" (in the section labeled "Targeting"). Then type a city, county, state or whatever you want in the textbox and click the blue Save button.

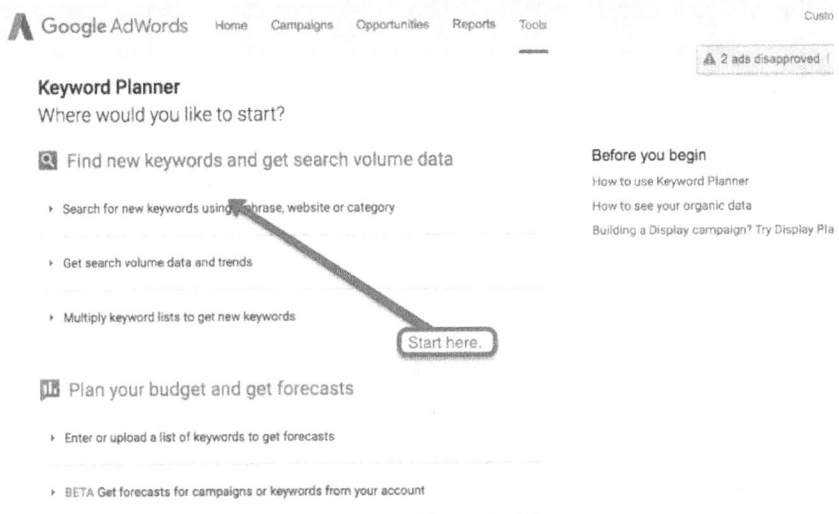

Look for keywords are that are highly relevant and have some history of traffic. Another criteria is the competitiveness of the keywords. Obviously, the lower the competition, the better. That will give you a better chance of ranking and a better chance of generating a conversion.

Traffic is the key. If you send me a list of 100 keywords with zero competition, I can have them all ranked number one in Google by next week. It would make the website owner feel good because he sees his website ranked in Google, but if those rankings don't actually drive any traffic to his website then he hasn't really accomplished anything.

Sometimes it is hard to identify keywords with a track record of clicks, so in that instance use your best judgment but focus on phrases that are highly relevant to your business.

Long tail versus high-volume

Keywords generally break out into two categories, and you should make use of both. The two types of keywords are high volume keywords and "long tail" keywords.

High-volume

These are the keywords that are most general and get the most traffic. These keywords are also usually very competitive. These keywords offer the possibility to drive a lot of traffic to your website but can be hard to get. They also don't convert as well.

Long tail

These are keywords that are much more specific. They will tend to be lower in volume than the keywords described above, but can be more profitable. They are easier to get and convert better.

Generally what you want to do is optimize your home page for the most broad, high volume keywords, but then optimize sub-pages of your site for the more specific long-tail keywords. That is where your blog can come into play.

So what's the next step after you have identified your keywords? At that point, you want to map those keywords to specific pages of your website, or build new pages for those keywords. You can't really optimize a web page for more than a couple of keywords. You've got to spread them out. I

So now let's talk about how to actually optimize your website.

On-page Optimization

The process of modifying a web pages title, copy and code so that the page has a better chance of ranking in a search engine is called "on-page optimization." Here are the main things you need to know about it.

Page URLs

Try to build out pages on your website that are optimized for specific keywords, and that use those keywords in the page URLs.

If you are a hotel located in Atlanta, Georgia, there could be a main page to your site focused on the types of rooms you offer with a URL like "/atlanta-hotel-tooms/".

Having the primary keyword for a web page in the URL for that page can help it rank for that keyword. Try to build out a catalog of pages on your website optimized for a variety of keywords, with the keywords in the URLs. Again, doing regular blog posts is a good way to do this. Using the Permalinks feature of WordPress helps accomplish this goal because a page will automatically have a URL that contains the page title.

Page Titles

The page title is the single most important thing about a web page as far as ranking in a search engine like Google. Use your main keyword for a page in the page title. If it makes sense, start the title with the keyword.

So if the target keyword for a page is "king size room with spa Austin", then the title of the page could be "King Size Room with Spa - Austin" or something along those lines.

This needs to be done on every major page of your website, not just your home page.

Copy

Next, you should try to use the keyword a couple of times in the copy on the page. Also try to use it in a header (text inside <H1> tags). There are three SEO criteria to keep in mind when writing your copy: word count, keyword density, and keyword prominence.

Word Count

This is just the total number of words in the copy. Generally speaking, more copy is better. Aim for a minimum of 300 words. If you can hit 500, especially on content-rich sub-pages, that is even better. If you can hit 1,000 words, that is dynamite.

Keyword Density

This is the number of times a keyword appears in the copy divided by the total number of words in the copy. Aim for a keyword density of 1%. But avoid making it appear artificial.

Keyword Prominence

This is how near the top of the copy your keyword appears. If you can make your keyword phrase the very first words on the page, that is great. But again, it should sound natural, and not forced. Try to get your keyword into the first paragraph or two if you can.

Meta Tags

After you have created a good title and copy for the page, the next step is to write a good meta description. This is basically a short paragraph that represents what Google will say about your website in the search results (although it doesn't have to use the meta description - sometimes it will just use text from the page).

The meta description is another thing that can influence how Google ranks your website, so it should be optimized for your target keyword for the page. However, it should read like a human written paragraph.

This process should be done on every major page of the site. Each page is optimized for one or two specific keywords.

Cross-linking

Try to sprinkle keyword links throughout the copy in the various pages. For instance, if you have a page about accommodations, then you could make the word "accommodations" on another page a link to that page.

Let's look at a hypothetical example of optimizing a web page to give you a more clear idea of what we're talking about.

Let's say you own a hotel in Asheville, North Carolina. You would need to do keyword research to identify what your top keyword should be. But it's probably safe to assume that your core number one keyword would be something like "Asheville, North Carolina Hotel".

In this case, you would want to have elements on your homepage similar to the following.

Page title: Asheville, North Carolina Hotel – [Name of Hotel]

At the top of the page, your keyword would be contained in a header, like this:

<H1>Asheville, North Carolina Hotel</H1>

The phrase "Asheville, North Carolina hotel" would be contained within the first paragraph or two of copy and would be in bold, like this:

<Strong >Asheville, North Carolina hotel</strong >

You would also want the keyword to be contained near the bottom of the copy on the page.

Try to have a minimum of 300 words in the main copy of the page, with your keyword used two to three times.

You will also need to use your keyword in the meta description for the page. That will look something like this:

<meta name = "description" content = "Asheville, North Carolina hotel [Name of Hotel] has a heated pool, free deluxe continental breakfast and many five star reviews."/>

As you can see, the meta-description is very similar to the page title, but is a little longer, allowing you to put in a little more detail. The meta description would appear in the head of the HTML document, and not in the body copy. It is not seen by the visitor.

The tags that you see around the information above (such as "title" used around the page title) are called HTML tags. One of the big advantages of using a platform like WordPress is that it is a WYSIWYG ("what you see is what you get") editor, meaning you can edit the content of your webpages without knowing HTML.

Now let's take a step back.

So what you have done above is optimize one page of your website for one keyword. However, it is very unlikely that all of the potential customers for your business will use the exact same keyword phrase. People think differently. They will use different words to search for your type of business.

But you don't have to just guess about that. Refer back to the section of this book about keyword research for details about how to use Google to find out what keywords people actually use to search for lodging in your market.

Site Maps

A site map is a page or file on your website that has a link to every page (or most pages). There are two types of site maps: HTML and XML.

HTML

An HTML site map is a publicly accessible page of your site that has links to all the other pages (or at least the pages you want people to find). This page is helpful both for humans as well as search engines. For your human visitors, it is just a quick way for them to find whatever page has the information they are looking for. For search engines, it makes it easier for them to explore the site and make a record of all the pages.

If you use WordPress for your site, you can install a plugin that will create your site map for you. However, as a word of warning, sometimes things get added to an automatically generated site map that you don't really want on there. Depending on how your WordPress theme works, there could be things that are actually parts of a page that the site map would consider a complete page. Make sure your sitemap only has links to legitimate pages that you want people and search engines to find.

XML

XML site maps are really just for search engines. XML is a markup language kind-of like HTML, but it is generally not really used as the main scripting language of a webpage. If you are using WordPress, you can install a plugin that will generate your XML site map for you.

In the section of this book about Google Webmaster, we go into detail about how to submit your XML site map to Google.

Links

The other side of SEO is creating links and building social media credibility for your website.

Having other websites link to your website is one factor that plays into your search engine ranking. All else equal, a website that has more or better quality links pointing to it will rank better. But quality is more important than quantity. If you can get CNN.com to link to your website, that is a very valuable link.

Of course, to get a link like that, your website needs to be associated with some kind of big time national story, or you need to be prepared to spend many thousands of dollars for the link. For the small business, it is just not feasible, so you will have to start with the basics and then use your creativity to find sources of links.

One strategy is to look at the link sources for your top online competitors with good search engine visibility.

Here is a free tool that you can use to discover some competitor links:

https://moz.com/researchtools/ose/

Type in the competitor website address and then look through the links for possible websites where you might also be able to get a link.

For a hotel, most of your links will likely come from travel-related directories, which we will discuss shortly.

Trust flow

For a number of years there was a concept very important in the search engine optimization process called "PageRank." PageRank is a sort-of ranking of importance that Google applies to web pages. What was useful about it is that that value could be passed around from one web page to another. So getting links from high PageRank web pages helped improve search rankings of the web page that is being linked to.

At the time of this writing, PageRank has given way to another concept called "Trust Flow." The idea behind Trust Flow is basically that you want websites to link to your website, and you want to link out to other websites, that are legitimate and highly relevant to the subject of your website.

Links from higher quality websites carry more weight and help improve your ranking more than lesser quality sites. Quality is more important than quantity.

It is a good idea for your lodging website to link out to other businesses in your area, especially other businesses that draw people into town – restaurants, shops and attractions. Become a hub for information about your town.

Next, you need to try and get some links pointing to your website from other relevant websites. This can be more tricky. The easiest way to start is with any kind of lodging-related directory you can find. You can also ask other local businesses to link to you. Look at it this way – anything that brings business into your town is good for you and for every other business in town. Be generous in helping promote (and link to) other complimentary businesses and they will very like be generous in promoting (and linking to) you in return.

Google WebMaster

You are going to need to set up a Google WebMaster account. This will give you some control over how Google finds and displays your website, as well as providing some valuable information that can help you with your website marketing.

To create your account, go to
https://www.google.com/webmasters.

If you don't already have a Google account, you will need to set one up. If you do already have a Google account, just click the sign in button. Once you are logged in to Google, visit the link above. To add your website, click the add a property button.

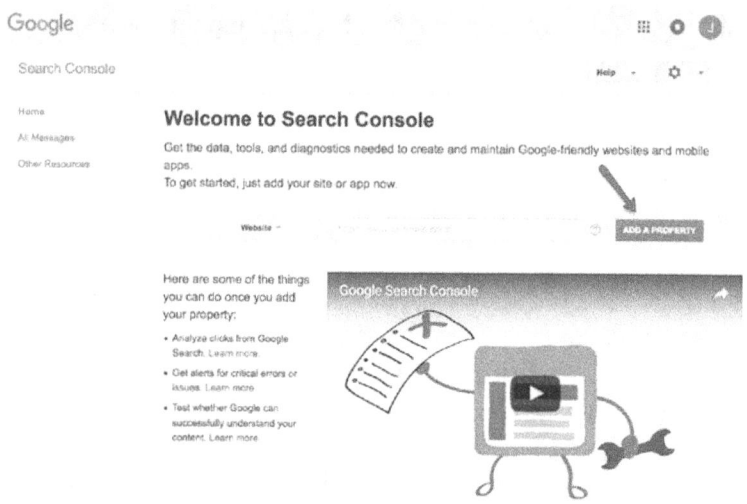

Before Google will allow you to use its WebMaster functionality, you have to prove that you are the owner or manager of the website. There are a few different ways that Google allows you to do this, but the quickest way is to upload a file that Google provides to your server. Then when Google finds the file, it knows that you have control of the site and are qualified to act as its Webmaster.

After getting your account set up, the first thing you should do is submit an XML sitemap. To do that, go to the Crawl/Sitemaps page and click the Add/Test Sitemap button. You will then provide the URL to your website sitemap. Which means, obviously, that there has to be an XML sitemap.

The easiest way to get that added to your website is to use a WordPress plugin. There is one called Google Sitemap Generator that is popular. If you don't use WordPress and don't have any way to automatically created a sitemap, you can create one manually using any text editor. Unless you are a real nerd, I would look for an automated way to do it.

Two things that Google shows you in your WebMaster account that are very useful to know are Google search impressions and clicks. It will also show you a list of keywords that were used in Google that resulted in impressions or clicks to your website.

It will show you your average ranking for the keyword and the click-through rate. If you see promising keywords in the list where your ranking is not that great, then those might be good candidates for SEO.

To clarify, an impression is when someone loads a search engine results page that has your website in the listings. An impression does not necessarily mean that the visitor clicked to your website. But you can't have clicks until you have impressions.

Google will not show you a complete list of all the keywords that generated impressions or clicks. I believe the general rule is that it won't show search phrases that consist of more than five words, but don't hold me to it. The point is that Google will show you many of the keywords people are using to find your website, but not all of them.

Your Google WebMaster account is also where you submit your XML site map. Go to the Crawl/Site Maps page and click the button to add your site map. You will then give Google the URL to your site map page. After some period of time, Google will process the site map and tell you if there were any problems with it.

Another important thing that Google will tell you is if it has had any crawl errors on your site. These are errors that Google has encountered while traveling through your site. You should work to fix these.

For example, if Google finds links on some pages that are incorrect, it will tell you. The cleaner your website is in terms of bad links or other mistakes, the better your chances of ranking well.

AMP

AMP, which stands for "Accelerated Mobile Pages," is a very new technology that can greatly improve the mobile user experience. What it does is send a stripped down, super fast version of a web page for mobile viewing. Google is able to detect if you have AMP installed, and it automatically links mobile search results to the AMP version of your site.

If you use WordPress, this is easily accomplished with use of an AMP plugin. When I first started testing this technology in WordPress, it worked perfectly the first time on two out of three websites. On the third one, it didn't cause any problems, but for some reason Google was unable to detect AMP.

If you don't use WordPress or some other platform where some smart people have already created something that will do AMP for you, then this is probably above your head. WordPress makes it easy.

Ranking Tracking

It is useful to track your rankings for your target keywords over time. Combined with your organic search traffic statistics, this will paint the picture if you are making progress in improving your search engine visibility.

It is not my intention to promote any particular third-party service, especially since I'm not making money from it, but I might as will mention MOZ (www.moz.com) as a good option for tracking your rankings. It is probably the number one service for this.

Another good option that I have used is Pro Rank Tracker (www.proranktracker.com).

The way any ranking tracking service works is that it is going to periodically perform a Google search for each of your target keywords to see where it ranks. This might be once per week or once per day. You can also specify if you want to track rankings on a nationwide basis or from a particular geographic area.

MOZ will also integrate with your Google analytics to display traffic statistics from organic search. It is convenient to have that data in the same interface as your search engine ranking data, because it sort of ties everything together. What you should see is that as your rankings improve, your organic search traffic improves as well.

These are paid services. If you want, you can just go to Google once per week and type your target keywords in yourself to see where you rank.

Word of caution: if you are logged into Google when you do this, your results will be distorted because Google will tailor the search results to your search history. So to get more accurate ranking results if doing this yourself, you need to make sure you're logged out of Google. The process of manually tracking the rankings can be a real pain, especially if you're tracking a large number of keywords. That's why it is convenient to you to use an automated service that does it for you.

Local SEO

When it comes to businesses that operate in a limited geographic market, things are done a little differently. This is a specific type of SEO called "local SEO."

The key components to a local SEO campaign are:

- Optimizing your website for local.

- Managing your Google Business account.

- Creating citations.

- Getting reviews.

Local Optimization

The whole point of local optimization is to make it very clear to Google that you are a legitimate business, what your business is, and where you are located. To accomplish these goals, do this:

- Use your page titles, meta descriptions and copy to make it very clear what your business is, as described in the on-page optimization section above.

- Put the street address and phone number in your website footer.

- Have a contact / location page on your site with your address and a Google map.

- If you have more than one location, each location should have its own page with complete contact information.

Google Business

A Google Business account is your key to getting your website to show up in the local section of a Google search results page, as shown below:

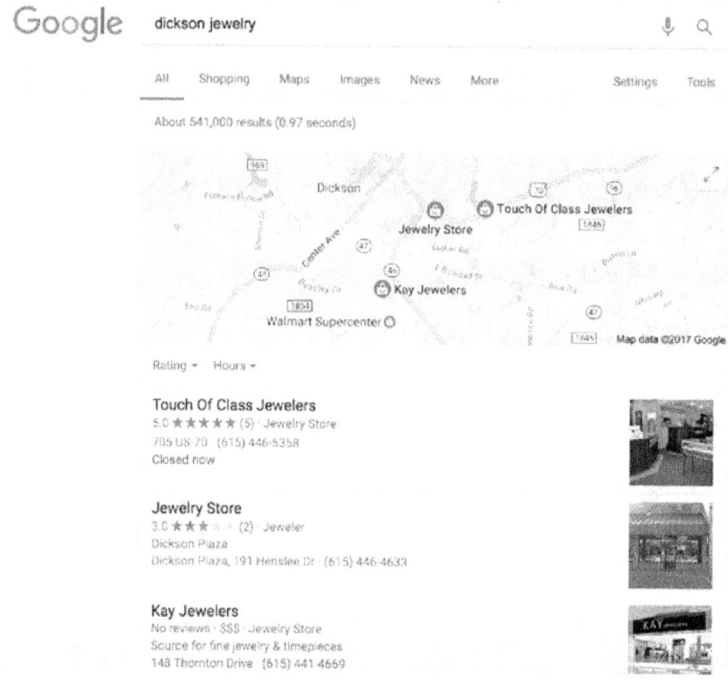

Google pulls that local business information from businesses that have Google Business accounts. If you don't have one, you're not going to show up.

Set up a Google business page by going to:

https://business.google.com/create

If you don't already have a Google account, that is step one. Click the Create account link and just follow the instructions to create a Google account.

Once your Google account is created, you will arrive at a welcome screen that has a blue button that says "Continue to Google My Business." If you don't see that button, use the web address shown above to get to the Google Business signup page.

The first page of the signup process is where you start telling Google all about your business - your name, address, phone, category, etc. Be very careful to type in all of your information correctly. The information you type in here should match what is shown on your website.

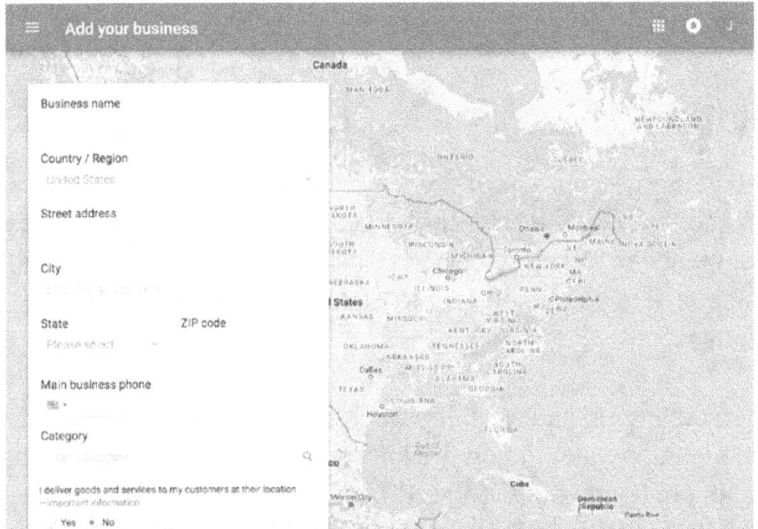

Google will then attempt to display your business address on a map and require you to click a button stating that you are authorized to manage the business and agree to Google's terms.

To complete the process, you will need a verification code that you get via a postcard from Google.

While you wait on the postcard from Google, you should go ahead and start filling out the details of your Google Business page. Use every option there is. Give your page a header background. Provide hours of operation, your website address and a phone number.

Add as many photos as it will let you. This is especially true for lodging businesses. High quality photography is important to create a good impression to potential customers.

Once your page is verified, which you can do after you receive the Google postcard, your property will be eligible to appear in Google local search results.

So now that you have a Google Business account set up with information that matches what is on your website, the next step is to start setting up some citations.

Citations

A citation is simply a reference to your business in some kind of local business directory or portal, along with an address for your business. It is very important to have these for local SEO purposes.

When setting up citations, the address and phone number shown in the citation must match the information shown on your website and as set up in your Google Business account. You need to make it very clear to Google exactly where you are located.

Here are some of the top general purpose directories at which you should add your business:

- www.Yelp.com

- www.BingPlaces.com

- www.CitySearch.com

- www.HotFrog.com

- www.YellowPages.com

- www.SuperPages.com

- www.Foursquare.com

For lodging businesses, you will also need to use:

- www.TripAdvisor.com

- www.Hotels.com

- www.Expedia.com

- www.Kayak.com

In addition, if there are directories of local businesses or lodging establishments, you should sign up for them as well.

Visit all of these websites and add your business. I would probably start with Yelp.

Yelp

To get your business listed in Yelp, you first have to see if it is in the Yelp directory, and then "claim" it if it is. To do that, go to the bottom of the page at https://www.yelp.com and click the link that says "Claim Your Business Page."

On the next page, type your business name in the appropriate box, make sure the correct city is selected, and click the Get Started button.

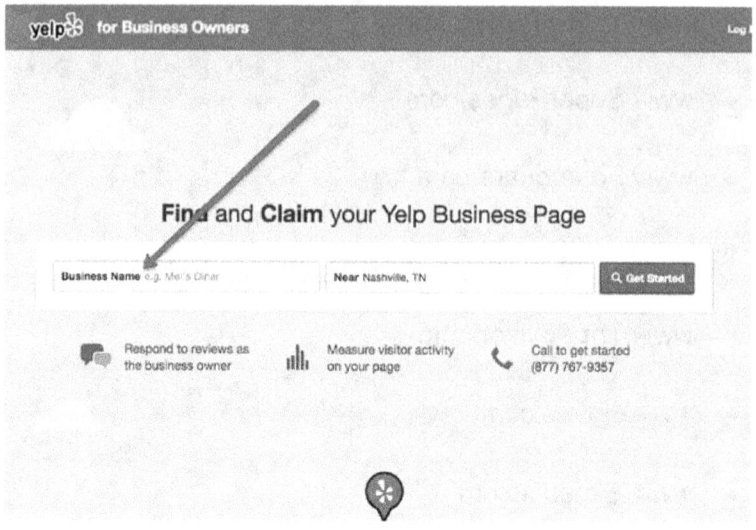

If you don't find your business, then at the bottom of the list of businesses that Yelp shows you on the next page, click the link that says "Add your business to Yelp."

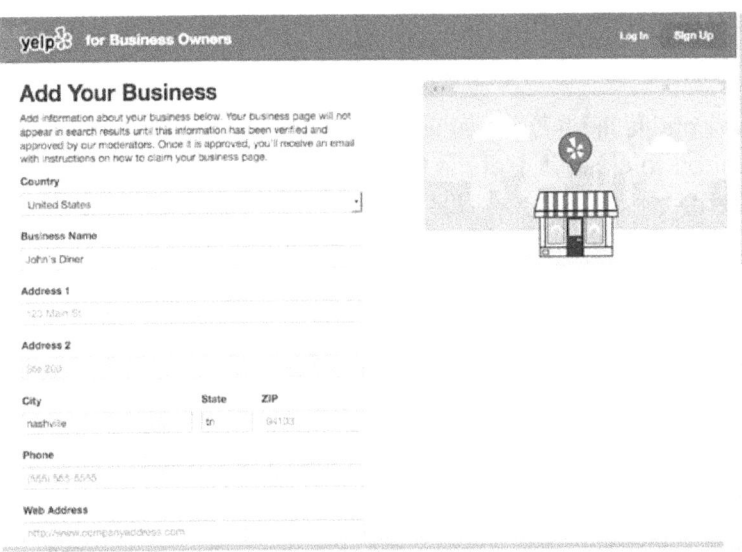

On the next screen, you will tell Yelp all about your business, similar to what you did when you were setting up your Google Business account. Again, make sure that the information you type in here matches EXACTLY what is shown on your website and in your Google Business account. EXACTLY.

I will say it one more time, in case you missed it: EXACTLY.

The process for signing up at the other local directory sites will vary. Some of them will require verification similar to Google. In some of them, like Yelp, your business could already be in the site, in which case you will have to claim it.

The above list is nowhere near a complete list of local directories, but if you start with this list, that will give you a real good start. If you add to this list over time, you will increase your total citations, thus helping improve your search rankings and potentially exposing your business to many new prospects.

I have not spent a whole lot of time on this section, as I leave it up to you to explore the above list of local portals. But do not overlook this. Creating citations is especially important for businesses operating at a local level.

Trip Advisor

Your hotel is likely already listed in Trip Advisor, in which case you will need to claim it. Here is the process as of the time this was written:

- Go to www.tripadvisor.com/owners.

- Search for your business name.

- When you find your business, click the Claim Your Business button.

- Log into Trip Advisor and follow the instructions to claim your listing.

Trip Advisor rankings are greatly affected by three factors:

- Review quality.

- Review quantity.

- Review recency.

Here are some tips for improving your ratings:

- Use every free option that there is and provide lots of detailed information.

- Add lots of photos.

- Add a video.

- Respond to negative reviews promptly.

- Have a positive attitude in your messaging on the site.

- Encourage your guests to leave reviews.

Expedia.com

Adding your property to Expedia will also add it to Hotels.com.

- Go to https://join.expediapartnercentral.com.

- Click the Join Us button.

- Follow the instructions to provide complete and detailed information about your property.

Kayak.com

- Go to www.kayak.com/hotelowner.

- Click the Add Hotel button.

- Click the Sign up button to create an account and follow the instructions from there.

Reviews

Google gives preference to business websites that have reviews. For hotels, they can also play a major role in generating bookings. Probably more than any other industry, positive reviews can make an incredible difference in the success of a hotel website. I would recommend that you try to get reviews from at least two general directories (your Google Business profile and your Yelp profile) as well as the most popular travel directories.

If you have a really lousy property and regularly cheat your customers, you will probably have reviews start popping up organically. It's not very hard to get negative reviews. Most people who go out of their way to talk about a business are doing so because they are unhappy.

To get positive reviews, you are going to want to ask your happy customers to review your property. I recommend giving them very specific instructions. I recommend giving them instructions similar to what follows.

Instructions for Leaving Social Media Reviews

We greatly appreciate you taking the time to follow these instructions to review our hotel online.

Google

Instructions for leaving a Google review:

1. Visit https://www.google.com. If you are not logged into Google, click the Sign In button in the upper right-hand corner.

2. If you do not have a Google account, follow the easy instructions to create one. Otherwise, type in your password to log into Google.

3. After logging in, do a Google search for "[your business name]."

4. On the right side of the screen, click the "Write a review" button.

5. Assign us a star rating (we would certainly appreciate 5!) and a comment in the "Describe your experience" section. Then click POST.

Yelp

Instructions for leaving a Yelp review:

1. Visit https://www.yelp.com/biz/[your Yelp business page].

2. Click the red Write a Review button.

3. On the next screen, leave us a number of stars and a review.

4. Click the red Sign Up and Post button and follow the instructions from there.

Trip Advisor

Instructions for leaving a Trip Advisor review:

1. Visit https://www.tripadvisor.com.

2. Type [hotel name] into the search box to search for our property.

3. Fill in the Write a Review form. Make sure to include:

   - Your rating.

   - Title.

   - Review text.

   - Type of trip.

- Date traveled.

4. Select the checkbox to certify that the review is based on a genuine travel experience and then press the Submit button.

Expedia

Expedia is a little different because its system sends an email to those who have booked a stay through Expedia. So in this case, you would just remind your visitors that if they booked through Expedia, they should look for an email invitation to submit a review.

Local Cross Promotion

It is a great idea to cross-promote with local restaurants, shops and attractions. In its simplest form, it can just be a relationship whereby you agree to place linked graphics or copy promoting your marketing partner and your partner does the same thing on its website.

A step up from simple cross-linking would be to create a package to promote to your website visitors that includes room booking plus discounts for whatever it is your cross-promotion partner sells. For example, maybe you cross-promote with a local restaurant so that your customers get a free dinner for two. You get the idea.

This type of idea is great not only because it creates incentives for your visitors to book a room, but it also helps with search engine optimization because it creates local links to your website.

Paid Search

You have probably noticed that if you do a search on Google, there are some listings at the top that have a little "ad" icon next to them. Those are paid ads. When someone clicks on one of those listings, that business is charged a fee for that click.

There are a couple of reasons you might want to pay for clicks. For one, it takes time to get your website in the organic listings. It can take months. Also, if you have both organic and paid listings on a search results page, that increases your search engine "shelf space." We'll talk about shelf space later.

The two major paid search platforms are Google AdWords and Bing Ads. Google obviously gets the most traffic, but Bing is worth trying as well and you might even save some money.

Now there are a few important concepts you need to understand.

Cost per Cilck

This is the amount of money you pay for one click. It won't be the same for every keyword, and it won't be the same every day. Paid search is basically an auction model where you bid a certain amount you are willing to pay for a click. However, your bid is not the only thing that determines when and where your ad will show up. Where your ad shows up is a function of many things, but some of the main things are:

- How much you bid for the keyword.

- How much competition there is for the keyword.

- How relevant the keyword is to its landing page.

- The click-through-rate of the ad.

Back in the olden days you used to be able to get clicks for a nickel. There ain't no nickel clicks anymore. These days, some businesses are spending $50+ on a click. That seems absurd, but it's not about the click cost - it's about your return on investment (discussed earlier) and cost per conversion (discussed below).

Cost per Conversion

Cost per conversion is what it costs you in dollars to get one conversion. A conversion does not necessarily have to be a sale, but for our purposes here let's just assume that it is. So if your hotel spends $1,000 on Google AdWords, and that generates 20 clients, then the cost per conversion would be $50.

The trick to knowing that is knowing how many sales the AdWords ads actually generated. Cost per conversion is calculated by dividing how much you spent in advertising by the number of sales the advertising generated.

Cost per conversion is very close related to return on investment.

If you recall, cost per conversion works like this: If you spend $100 on Google AdWords clicks, and as a result do $500 in bookings, then you have a return on investment of 400% ($4 in profit for every $1 spent in advertising).

Google AdWords

To get started with Google AdWords, visit https://adwords.google.com.

You will first have to log in with your Google account. If you don't have a Google account…have you been paying attention? Go sign up for a Google account…NOW!

WARNING: Google is very good at getting your money. If you don't know what you're doing, you can spend a lot and not get much out of it. Be careful. Work with an AdWords professional if you don't feel comfortable with this stuff.

Campaigns and Ad Groups

Your AdWords account will divide out into logical groupings called campaigns and ad groups. A campaign consists of ad groups. An ad group is a combination of keywords and ads.

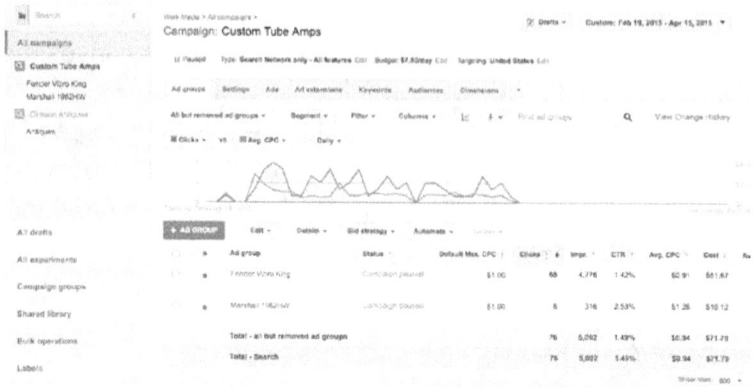

All of the ads and keywords in a particular ad group should be very related. For example, you might have keywords that break out into the following groupings:

- Hotel

- Downtown

- Luxury

So you would want to create a separate ad group for each of those keyword groupings:

- Hotel ad group – keywords and ads that reflect people just looking for a hotel

- Downtown ad group – keywords and ads that reflect those looking specifically for a downtown hotel

- Luxury ad group – keywords and ads that reflect those looking specifically for a luxury hotel

The more closely related an ad is to the exact information the searcher is looking for, the more effective it will be. That's why if I am looking for a downtown hotel, you should how me an ad that specifically talks about "downtown hotel."

The campaign level is a higher level up than ad groups and represents a broader grouping. All of the ad groups within a campaign share the total campaign budget. So you might put all of the above ad groups into the same campaign, or you might put them into separate campaigns if you want them to have separate budgets.

Your geographic targeting also happens at the campaign level. So if you need to allocate separate budgets for different geographic markets or target those markets with different ads, then you will need to use separate campaigns for those markets.

There are a number of different ways to tell Google how much you want to pay for each click. You can let Google set your bids for you if you specify that you want to get as many clicks as you can within your budget. In that case, Google will automatically move bids up and down to accomplish that goal. Sometimes this works well. However, there have been times when I was very unsatisfied with the results I got from this technique. So at that point I would just set the bids myself manually.

Another thing that I have found about letting Google set bids is that Google tends to bid for very high positioning – ads that appear in the top one or two positions. This can be expensive. You can get lower cost clicks by bidding for lower positions.

Starting out, what you might want to do is set your bids to a level at which you are comfortable and then make adjustments over time as you go.

Google can also adjust your bids based on conversion data. This actually brings me to an important topic, which is that you can be much more effective with paid search (and all marketing) if you have a way to track conversions. So let's talk about it.

Conversion Tracking

You need to know when someone visits your site and takes some kind of action. That action can be filling out a contact form, calling you on the phone, or (best of all) booking a room.

Room booking is definitely the main conversion event you need to be concerned with. My discussion here is going to be based on using Google Analytics, although there are other options.

When someone finishes booking a room on your website, she needs to be redirected to a confirmation / thank you page. That is where the conversion tracking code is located. This allows Google to tell you that a transaction took place and where it came from.

The room booking system that your website uses may have configuration options that allow you to set conversion tracking variables right from your booking backend. In that case, you would not worry about a confirmation page. These are technical details that your website designer will need to work through.

AdWords Conversion Tracking Script

To find the conversion tracking script in Google AdWords, click Tools/Conversions on the top main menu. Then click the +Conversion button.

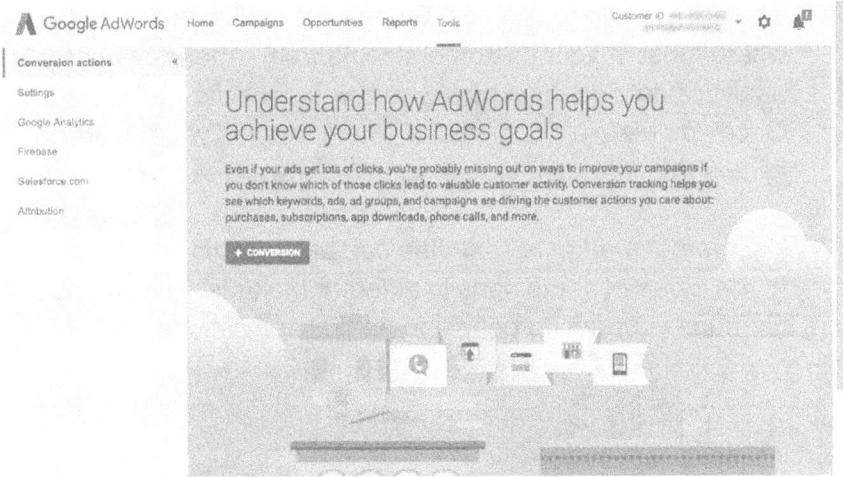

There are a few different types of conversions you can track, but the two you will likely use are Website conversions (form submissions or online sales) and Phone calls (when someone calls you after seeing your ad).

For phone conversions, you will need a call tracking number. This is a phone number that is different from your main number but redirects to your business. This allows you to track conversions because you will know that those calls originated from your AdWords click.

Select the type of conversion you want to track and follow the instructions. There are a lot of different options here and ways to set up your conversions. I don't really want to bog down this book with a lot of technical instructions on setting up conversions. Again, if you're not sure what you're doing, consult the help of an AdWords pro.

Geographic Targeting

You need to tell Google exactly where you want your ad to run. Hotels are a little different from other types of businesses because most of your target market is going to be OUTSIDE of the market where you are physically located. Initially, it might be hard to know where you need to run ads. Study your bookings so you know where most of your customers come from. Analyze your website analytics data so you know where your website traffic comes from. Once you have a good idea of where most of your business comes from, that should tell you where you need to run your ads.

Your target market is set in the campaign settings. This allows you to run different campaigns in different markets. This is one way to fine-tune your ads to people in particular locations.

Keywords

Keywords are the search terms that should trigger your ads. Typical keywords for a hotel will be like the following:

- [the name of your hotel]

- hotels [your city]

- [your city] hotel

So if your hotel is located in Topeka, Kansas, examples of good keywords to target would include "hotels Topeka Kansas" and "Topeka Kansas hotel."

As discussed above, your keywords should be segregated into highly related groupings. Those then become your ad groups.

How closely the search query has to match the keyword in order to trigger an ad is determined by the keyword match type.

Match Types

The keyword match type determines how closely the user's search query must match the keyword in your account in order for Google to show your ad.

The three main types of keyword match types are:

- Exact match

- Broad match

- Phrase much

Exact Match

Exact match means that Google will only show your ad if the search query used matches your keyword exactly. This is the safest kind of match type to use. However, you may end up limiting the number of times your ad appears.

Broad Match

Broad match means that Google will show your ad if the search query is similar to, but not necessarily the same as, your keyword. Using broad match keywords may greatly increase the number of times your ad appears in search results, but it can also result in many more non-relevant matches.

Phrase Match

Phrase much means that the user's search query must contain your keyword exactly as it is, but can also have additional words before or after it. If the keyword is "Indianapolis hotel", then the search queries "good Indianapolis hotel" and "Indianapolis hotel downtown" would both trigger the ad.

So what type of match type should you use for the keywords in your account? I usually like to start with mostly exact match. And then if I'm just not getting enough traffic, I will begin adding broad match or phrase match keywords as well.

One strategy I have used a lot is to have each keyword in my account set as both exact match and phrase match. If there is an exact match on the keyword, then that is the match that Google should make. I should get the best click cost with an exact match.

I probably use phrase match the most after exact match. There are a million different ways that somebody might be looking for somewhere to stay, so phrase match lets me capture many more possible variations than exact match.

If possible, I avoid broad match because of the much greater chance at irrelevant keyword matches. But if you find that you're just not getting enough ad impressions, then broach match ads will pick up the traffic.

Google will show you the exact search phrases that have resulted in clicks. So what you can do is go through that list periodically and add attractive phrases as keywords in your account if they are not already. To see this information, click Dimensions, then change the View dropdown list to "Search terms."

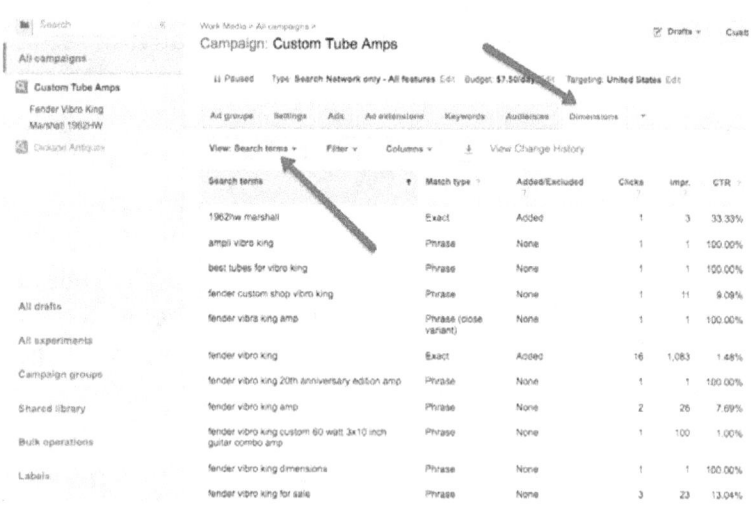

Dayparting

Another way you can fine-tune your account is to only run ads at certain times of the day. This is called dayparting. Initially, it will be difficult to know if there is any advantage to doing this. What you want to do is look at your data over time to see if you have better performance at certain times of day, and then start running ads more during those times.

Similarly, you may find that it is more productive to run ads on certain days of the week. Or maybe you want to decrease your click cost on the weekend. These are all things that can be adjusted.

AdSense (Content Network) Ads

There is another way you can use Google to advertise your business, which is by placing ads on websites that are part of the Google AdSense network. This is a little different because you are placing graphical ads on websites that are relevant to your target market, but not Google search results pages.

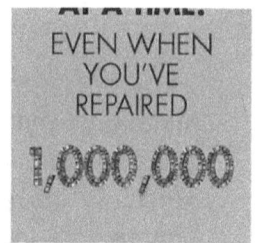

Google image ad on a Ford Mustang fan site.

The websites where your ad appears will be private websites run by various people who have signed up for the AdSense program to make money on advertising.

You will find that the click-through-rates of content network ads are less than that from search engine results page ads, but you often also pay less for those clicks. Ultimately, the thing that matters most is your cost per conversion and return on investment. Where are you getting the most conversions at the best cost? It might be search ads or it could be content network ads.

You can run content network ads through the same campaigns you run search ads. But I would suggest you keep them separate and run content network ads in their own campaigns. When setting up a new campaign, you specify if you want to run ads in search, on content network sites, or both. Just pick one or the other.

Dimensions

Pieces of data like the time of day and day of week are referred to as "dimensions" in Google AdWords. There are a bunch of different dimensions you can analyze. We have talked some about the time dimensions, although hour of day and day of week are not the only ones you can look at. You can break it down by month, hour, year, etc.

Some of the other things you can look at include geography, which breaks down all the way to the ZIP code level, the search terms used in your account (which are not the same as the keywords set up in your account), and the final destination URLs at which the visitors arrive.

Google wants to make money (and they are very good at it) but they also want you to be successful, so they provide you with all kinds of information you can use to improve your account performance. You're going to need to spend some time in your account to learn how to analyze this data and use it to make adjustments.

Ad Extensions

Add extensions are very useful because they allow you to add additional information to your ad, or just make them bigger. I will briefly run through a couple of them.

Call Extension

Call extensions add your phone number to your ads. For hotels, or any kind of business that takes reservations, this is obviously a good idea. Some people would just rather talk to someone on the phone than use a website. Using this extensions adds the phone number to your ad without taking space away from copy.

Site Links Extension

The site links extension allows you to add links to specific pages of your website to your ad. Google doesn't always show these, but sometimes it will. For example, you could choose to show site links for a page that describes your rooms, a page that gives background about the property, a page that provides contact information, and the page to book a room.

Call Out Extension

Call out extensions allow you to add a call out such as "Book your room now," "Make an appointment now" or "Big sale this weekend." I suggest you come up with a reason to have a call out. It will make your ad bigger and draw attention to it.

Review Extension

Review extensions allow you to post text from a third-party review as part of your ad. However, this needs to be a review that is live on a third-party website that Google can verify. An example would be reviews on Yelp.

All of these ad extensions make your ad physically bigger on the search results page, increasing their chance at getting noticed. They also provide more information to the user. I would suggest you spend some time on these things and figure out how to use the extensions that make sense for your ads.

Remarketing

Remarketing is a very powerful concept. Have you ever noticed how if you visit a particular website or business, afterwards you will start seeing ads for that business following you around on other websites? That is remarketing.

Conversion rates and cost per conversion for remarketing ads can be outstanding. Remarketing ads only appear on content network websites. They are not search engine ads.

The specifics of setting up a remarketing campaign are beyond the scope of this book. If you have trouble figuring out how to do it based on Google's instructions, it is probably worth consulting an AdWords professional.

Here is the Google support page with instructions on how to set up remarketing:

https://support.google.com/adwords/answer/3210317?hl=en

Needless to say, remarketing is a powerful tool because it takes advantage of a basic marketing principle, which is that advertising is much more effective when exposed multiple times to its audience.

Negative keywords

Negative keywords are keywords that should prevent an ad from being displayed. They help make sure your budget is used for the most relevant search queries. For example, let's say your hotel does not allow pets. Using "pet friendly" as a negative keyword will prevent your ad from showing to those looking for a pet friendly hotel.

Negative keywords can be set up at the campaign level or as a shared library item, which allows you to use the same negative keywords across different campaigns. The key to making effective use of negative keywords is to keep an eye on the search terms that are bringing traffic to your website.

You should regularly monitor your search terms (from the Dimensions section of AdWords) to identify words that should be added as keywords, and those that should be added as negative keywords.

Google Hotel Ads

Going beyond standard Google AdWords ads, Google offers another type of advertising specifically for hotels. This allows you to inject your hotel into Google's own hotel booking engine that appears when conducting a hotel search.

For example, if I search for "Nashville hotel," this is what I see at the time of this writing:

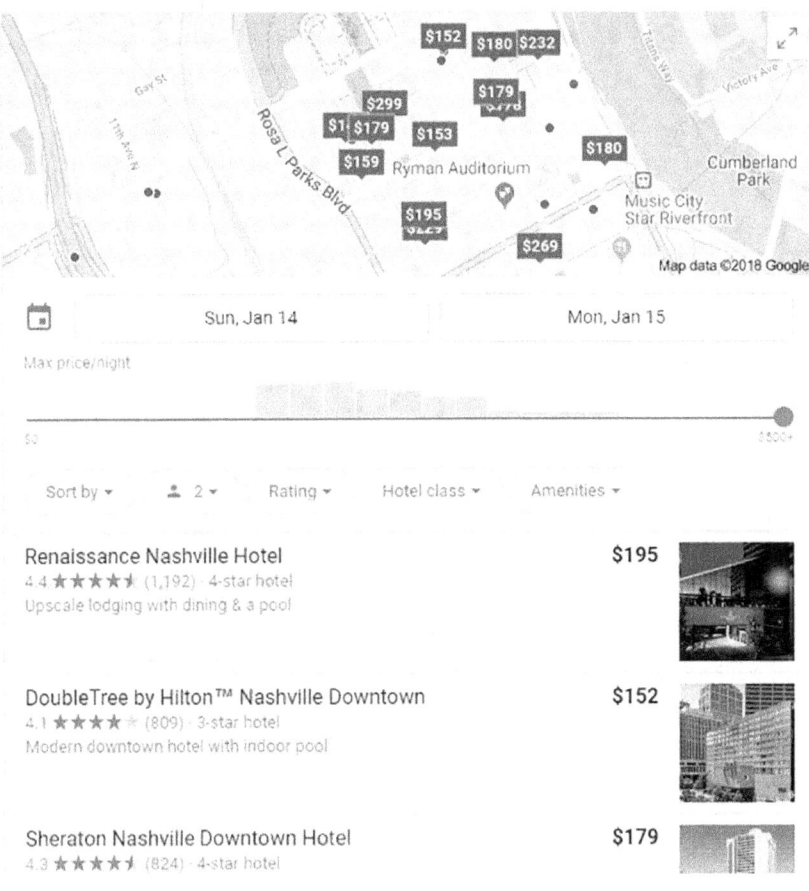

| Sun, Jan 14 | Mon, Jan 15 |

Max price/night

$0 $500+

Sort by ▾   👤 2 ▾   Rating ▾   Hotel class ▾   Amenities ▾

Renaissance Nashville Hotel $195
4.4 ★★★★⯪ (1,192) · 4-star hotel
Upscale lodging with dining & a pool

DoubleTree by Hilton™ Nashville Downtown $152
4.1 ★★★★☆ (809) · 3-star hotel
Modern downtown hotel with indoor pool

Sheraton Nashville Downtown Hotel $179
4.3 ★★★★⯪ (824) · 4-star hotel

Do you notice the way the screen has options that let you narrow down your hotel options? At the bottom of this short list is a link to view the entire list. If I click that, I see this:

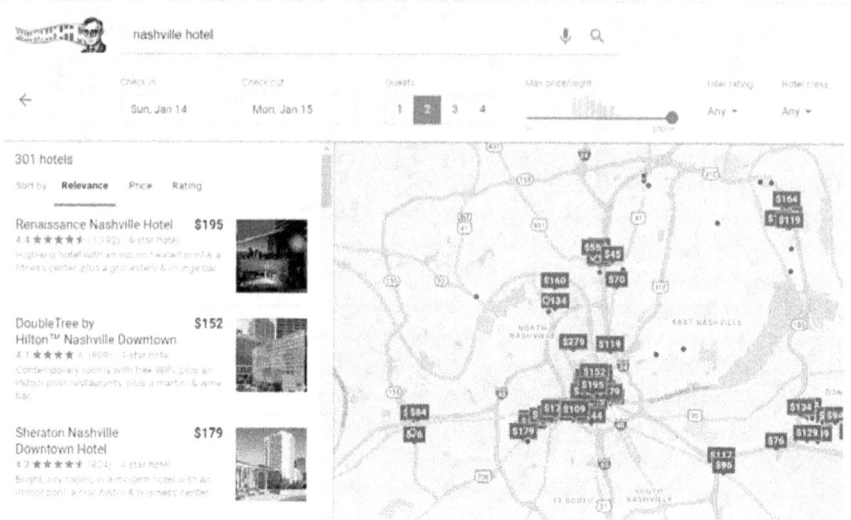

Now it shows a map of the city with markers showing where the various hotels are, along with little price markers. And there are still various options at the top to let you narrow down your search.

To get your hotel shown in this list, you use a service called Google Hotel Ads.

To get started with these types of ads, visit https://www.google.com/ads/hotels/. To use this service, you will have to work with an agency designated as an "authorized Hotel Ads Integration Partner." This is a small group of agencies that have been invited by Google to provide this service to the hotel industry.

This is a complex process that involves setting various XML files (a type of data file) that provides up-to-date information to Google about your hotel, your rooms, your prices, etc. There is really no way to set this service up yourself, so I am going to defer to the list of agencies listed on the page referenced above. Consult with those guys to get signed up for the program.

Bing Ads

You can also try Bing Ads. Bing includes ads on both the Bing search engine as well as Yahoo. The two together account for about 10% of the search market, compared to about 80% for Google. However, 10% can still be a whole lot of people. Now, at the local level, it may not represent enough traffic to make any difference. But you really don't know until you try it. And if it works, you might find that your Bing traffic is more cost effective than your Google traffic.

To try Bing, go to https://advertise.bingads.microsoft.com.

Bing works pretty much the same way as Google AdWords, so I'm not going to go into any more detail about it here. Not all features will be the same, but the big stuff is. Your account will be divided out into campaigns and ad groups, with your ads and keywords being contained in the ad groups. If you are running AdWords ads, you can port your Google ads over to Bing to start with.

The trick is to make sure you measure performance, whether you're running Google ads, Bing ads, or anything else. If you don't have statistics for each different technique, then you won't really know what works and what doesn't.

Split Testing

One of the biggest advantages of paid search marketing is that it allows you to perform split testing of ad copy and other marketing variables in a very cost-effective way. It is possible that one advertisement for your product or service could greatly outperform what works best is called split testing.

Split testing has been done for many years, but it has often been a very expensive procedure. With Google AdWords and other similar online advertising platforms, split testing is very simple because all you have to do is create multiple ads for your ad groups, and the advertising platform will automatically rotate the ads for you.

One thing to caution against: ultimately, conversion data is the most important thing you should use to judge your performance. Getting lots of clicks is great, but getting conversions is way better. For that reason, I suggest that you set your ad groups to rotate ads evenly.

Depending on your settings, Google will use click-through-rates to automatically spend more on ads that have a better click-through-rate. But it could very well be that another ad that has a lower click-through rate has a higher conversion rate, in which case Google would cause you to spend more on the lower performing ad.

In the end, you need to use your own eyeballs and brain to determine what is working and what is not, and make account changes accordingly. Avoid just automating everything so that Google makes all the decisions for you. I do believe that Google wants you to be successful...but Google is also very good at getting your money regardless of account performance.

Paid Search Landing Pages

Most people link their paid search ads to one of the regular pages of their site. However, you might get better performance if the landing pages, or destination URLs, for your paid search ads are not the same as the regular pages of your website. You need to think about this strategically.

If a person clicks on your ad and arrives at your home page, he may not immediately find the information he is looking for. You need to send that visitor to exactly the page that has the information he wants.

You need to think like a direct marketer. Direct marketing usually involves presenting your prospective customer with a specific offer. It's not so much "Hey, my business is great," but more like "Hey, my business is great. Come see me now and save $50." The difference is that in direct marketing you are presenting a specific offer. Often multiple offers are split test to see what is most persuasive.

Remember that with paid search marketing, you are paying for every click to your website. Therefore, you may have better results by using some kind of specific offer. In fact, one good strategy is to only give the user a single option of what to do on a landing page.

Conversion tracking scripts will tell you what works best – what ads, keywords, landing pages, dimensions, etc. This is a step up in terms of technical difficulty because some programming has to take place in order for the website to pass the e-commerce information to the script. That's another one of those things that I'm not really going into details about here. It can often vary based on the particular booking engine your website uses. Seek the help of a qualified website developer if you need someone to add this functionality to your website.

Another thing that you want to measure is performance from desktop computers versus mobile devices. Some businesses (such as hotels) lend themselves very well to mobile devices. And it is certainly no secret that more and more search activity is taking place on mobile devices, often via voice search.

So if your data shows that you are performing better on mobile devices, or vice versa, you should adjust your bids appropriately to account for that. Google allows you to adjust your bids so that you spend more on the type of device that works best for you.

To adjust bids for different devices, click Settings, then Devices. Then click the little dash in the "Bid adj" column for the device you want to adjust, as shown below.

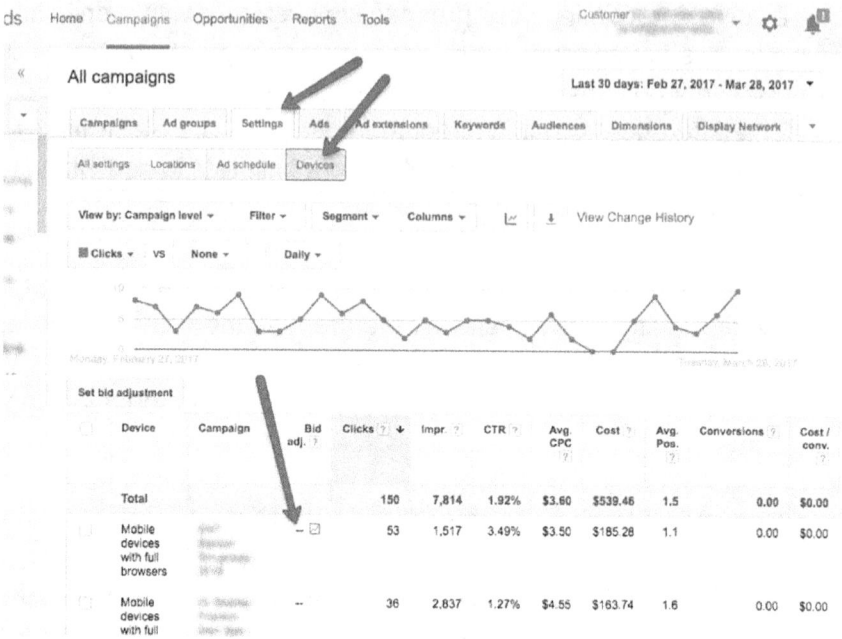

You are going to need to make sure that your website is mobile friendly. Really, your website needs to be mobile friendly anyway, but especially if you are spending money to drive traffic to it from mobile search.

Social Media

Another big part of the Internet marketing equation is using social media, especially Google+ and Facebook. I don't really know anyone who uses Google+ for pleasure the way that people use Facebook. However, in terms of affecting search visibility in Google, Google+ is more important. This makes sense when you consider that Google+ is, obviously, owned by Google.

Facebook provides the best opportunity for a local business to push its marketing message in front of prospective customers in its local area. I have also found it to be a lower cost source of paid clicks than Google. It can be a very effective marketing platform for hotels.

I don't do a whole lot with Twitter. I don't think it is as useful for hotels as Facebook and Google+, but it can certainly be effective if you have time for it. For our purposes here, I am going to focus mostly on Facebook and Google+ as I believe they are the social media sites most important for the lodging industry.

The approach I suggest for your hotel social media campaign is to post a variety of different types of content:

- Articles or blog posts posted to your website.

- Reposts from other related but non-competing social media profiles.

- Interesting, humorous or holiday-related "memes".

- Interesting news articles related to your location.

- Information about upcoming events.

Be proactive in liking and sharing content. This not only builds good will but it creates content for your own updates.

As you follow people and businesses, you will begin to like their updates and share anything interesting on your own timeline. People on Facebook are dying to have their updates liked and shared. When you do this, you create a connection with that person.

You also want other people and businesses sharing your content. This effect is magnified if it involves businesses that are complementary to yours. Local restaurants and attractions are great businesses to cross-promote on Facebook pages and the like.

This is a process that needs to be done on an ongoing basis. Once a week is not enough. Try to do some kind of update every day, even if it is just sharing someone else's update.

Pre-scheduling your posts can make your life easier. This is a good way to make sure that your account stays updated. Memes (discussed below), cartoons, photos and other interesting visual items are good candidates for this type of pre-scheduling.

Video is something that works well. And these days, at least for social media updates and such, you really don't need anything more than your phone. Now, if you make video a cornerstone of your marketing in general, then you will want to invest in some good quality video recording and audio equipment. However, for doing Facebook updates, all you have to do is hit the record button and start recording. I'm assuming you have a smart phone for video recording and upload. If not, get one. It's hard to do local online marketing these days without a smart phone.

I would keep videos short, maybe two or three minutes or less, unless you really have something fascinating to tell your viewers about.

Contests are also a great way to spread your message on Facebook. It used to be very restricted how you could do this, requiring some kind of paid Facebook app most of the time. Luckily, a while back Facebook relaxed the rules so that you can now simply ask people to like a post in order to enter a contest.

So now a contest is as simple as posting some kind of interesting content, and telling your Facebook friends that all they all they have to do is like the post to enter. I believe Facebook technically does not allow sharing of the content as a requirement, but you are certainly allowed to request that your friends share the post.

I usually state that you must both like and share an update to enter the contest. Then I request that you let me know you entered in the comments to the update. The problem is that you can't actually see everyone who shares your updates, so if you ask people to let you know they did it, at least you have that to go by.

Running a contest like this is not all that scientific. To pick a winner, take the list of people who liked the update (again, you won't really know who shared it and who didn't) and pick a winner at random.

Obviously, you need to have some kind of prize that is attractive enough to cause people to want to enter the contest. This could be something like a free weekend at your property, or some kind of unrelated prize. It just needs to be something people would like to have.

There are still third-party apps that can allow you to set up a more sophisticated contest, including automated random picking of a winner. You will probably need something like that if you want to do anything more advanced than what I discussed above. My point is that getting started with contests is as simple as asking people to like a post in order to enter.

One point to emphasize when promoting a contest is that, at least initially, odds are good. If only 30 or 40 people enter the contest (which would not be unusual for a new account), then those who enter have much better odds than the typical contest.

Facebook events are another way to drive traffic to a business. If you have an open house, party or some other type of event, you can promote it as an event on Facebook.

The last thing I'll say about your Facebook updates is that they should be interesting and visual. Don't just do text updates. As people are scrolling through their Facebook account, they may very likely pass over something that is straight text because it doesn't pop out at them. So it should contain an image or video, even if most of the content revolves around text. I suggest using an image with every single Facebook update.

Now, as for this whole knowing and liking thing, I am going to give you some seriously good advice right now. Honestly, I should redirect you to a link on my website where you are forced to pay $50 to download a PDF of instructions.

However, because I am feeling generous, I'm going to go ahead and give you this advice for free (the price of this book notwithstanding).

Here it is:

Be nice.

Be friendly.

Be honest.

Be helpful.

That's it. It's amazing how effective being nice is as a marketing strategy. People like to help people who they like. So if you are known as a friendly, nice person, people are more likely to help your business grow.

Be conversational. If your Facebook followers post messages, respond accordingly. Say things.

Also, place buttons on your site to make it easy for your visitors to like your content. If you use WordPress, you can use a plugin to automatically add these buttons to your pages. One that I have used that I like is called Social Media and Share icons (Ultimate Social Media), but there are lots of other options. Just go to the Add Plugins page and search for "social media share."

If you don't use WordPress, you can still install code to add share buttons to your site manually, but it's a lot more work. To manually add a share button for Facebook, visit https://developers.facebook.com/docs/plugins/share-button. This is somewhat advanced, so you may have to work with your website developer on its implementation.

Google+

You will want to create a Google+ account for your property. To get started, go to https://plus.google.com/.

I am assuming you have already created a Google business page for your business as explained earlier. If not, go do that first. Then come back and create a Google+ account.

Configure the account completely, using every option there is. Give it a background header. Upload as many photos as it will let you. Add as much information as you possibly can. When someone visits your Google+ page, it should look complete.

Begin immediately to post updates in your Google+ account. If you publish articles and blogs on your website, then every time you do an update, that should be used as an update for Google+.

Anytime you find an interesting article, something to link to, or something you can comment on that is related to your market or might be interesting to your followers, use it as an update.

After you have something to see on your account, start following other users of Google+. Many of them will follow you back in return. You should look for other users who are in the position of possibly needing your services or who are possible referral sources.

You should also put a plus button on your website so that anyone who is logged into Google can plus your website. This is very important for helping drive up search engine rankings. Google plus ones are very valuable.

Facebook

Next, you should create a Facebook Page for your business. If you don't already have a personal Facebook account, you should set that up first. Then you can use that account to create your business Page. In Facebook, business Pages do not have their own login. Your login will be your personal account, and then you will access your business through that.

To set up your business page, log into Facebook and then go to https://www.facebook.com/pages/create.

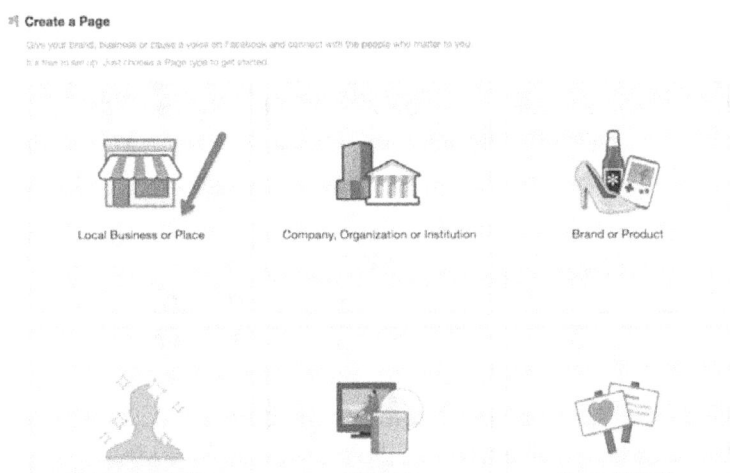

Create a Page

Give your brand, business or cause a voice on Facebook and connect with the people who matter to you.
It's free to set up. Just choose a Page type to get started.

Local Business or Place   Company, Organization or Institution   Brand or Product

Artist, Band or Public Figure   Entertainment   Cause or Community

Facebook will have you select the type of business you have. You will select the "Local Business" option. Then just follow the instructions.

Give your page an attractive header image and provide complete information about your property - location, hours of operation, etc. Add some photos, or videos if you have them. Even if you are just starting out, you need to have a Page that is attractive and interesting to visitors. Once the Page is set up, it is time to start doing updates.

Some of the keys to Facebook are:

- Post interesting content on a regular basis.

- Share content from other users.

- Respond quickly to questions or comments posted by other users, as appropriate.

- When you do an update that promotes your property, use Facebook's advertising system to boost it for more impressions. It is very difficult to build a Facebook following without boosting your posts. We will discuss this more later.

- Follow and like other people and business Pages that are in a position to refer you business or help you in any way. Do this as your business, and not as yourself.

Follow the Pages of complementary businesses such as tourist attractions and restaurants. Comment on their posts. Encourage them to follow you back. Occasionally repost their updates.

It is important that you do things in Facebook as your business, and not just as you personally. This includes following other businesses and liking, commenting, or sharing their updates. It is not extremely obvious how to do this, and Facebook often changes how this process works.

To like another business Page as your business, click the three little dots beneath its header graphic and select to like as your page. If you manage multiple pages, like I do, then you will need to select the particular page you wish to like as.

If this has changed by the time you read this, don't blame me. Blame FaceBook and its management who can never make up their minds about how this stuff is supposed to work.

You need to view the Facebook feed of the business Pages that you follow as your business. To do that, at the time of this writing, go to your Facebook home page by clicking the Facebook logo. Then click the Pages Feed link on the left-hand menu. You may have to click the View More link to expand the menu to see it. You will then see the updates of all the pages you follow.

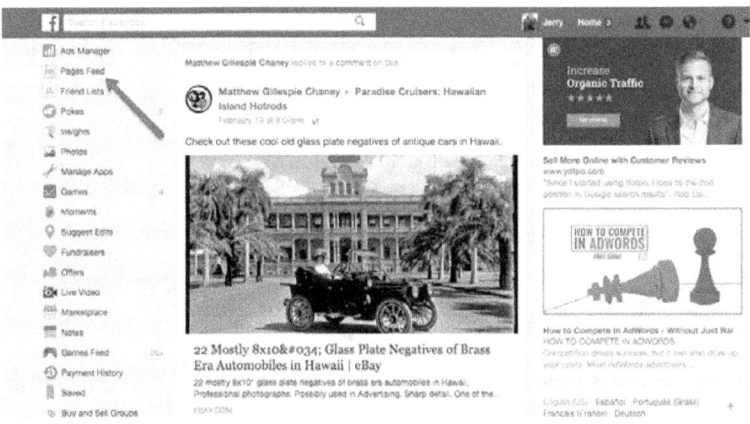

To like or comment on an update from another Page, click the small arrow at the lower right-hand corner, and then select your business name. Then your like or comment will be recorded as coming from your business.

One point I would also like to make about Facebook is that you should not put all your marketing effort into promoting your Facebook page. You do not own your Facebook page – Facebook does. If Facebook goes away or decides you can't have a Page anymore, you're screwed. Ultimately, you want people coming to a property that you own. That would be your own website.

Kickstart Your Facebook Page

Here are some instructions to give to anyone you know to help kickstart the performance of your business Facebook Page

1. Like and follow the Page.

91

a. After logging into Facebook, visit the Page by going directly to the Page URL, which will be something like: https://www.facebook.com/[page name].

b. Click the Like button beneath the header image.

2. Recommend the Page.

a. Click the Recommend button beneath the header image.

b. In the textbox that appears, type some reason for recommending the Page.
c. Click Post.

3. Invite your Facebook friends to like the Page.

a. Click the little button with 3 dots beneath the header image.

b. From the dropdown list, click Invite Friends.

c. Customize the message in the textbox however you want, or leave it as is.

d. Select the friends from your friend list you would like to invite.

e. Click Send Invites.

4. When you see [your hotel] updates in your news feed, like and share the update.

a. Click the Like button beneath the update.

b. Click the Share button beneath the update to share it to your own timeline.

5. Use your Facebook Page URL in marketing material whenever possible.

Memes

You may not know what the word "meme" means. But you have definitely seen them. A meme is really any piece of media that gets passed around. Memes are those cute little graphics or funny pictures with humorous or philosophical sayings that people love to share on their social media accounts.

They can be a good way to feed your social media accounts with easy content that people might be prone to liking or sharing. You should not rely on them as your only source of content, but they are a good way to keep some kind of content flowing and to encourage others to share your stuff.

You can go to Pinterest and search for funny related images or cartoons. Or do a Google Image search. If you use Google, I would use the Search Tools option to select images that are labeled for reuse. And you can always purchase stock photography as well. You can even pre-schedule a number of updates using those images.

There are also programs you can use that will create memes for you by combining an image of your choice with whatever words you want to use. An example of this would be the image of a famous person combined with a quote from that person.

One advantage to creating your own meme is that you can brand it with your own logo or other material. If people are going to pass something around via your social media accounts, you might as well get credit for it.

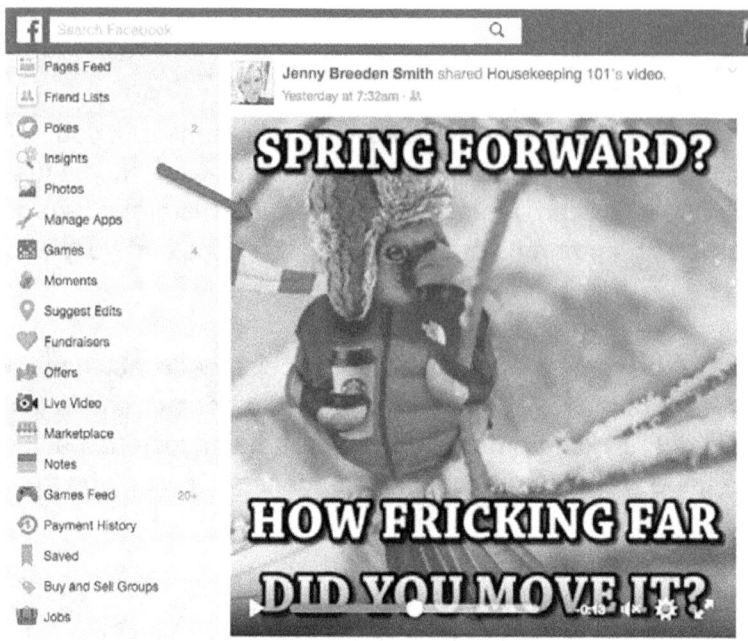

Going viral

Sharing is the key to making social media work. You've probably heard the expression "going viral." This basically refers to the act of multiple people sharing some piece of information to their social media accounts, and then multiple other people sharing it from those accounts, and so on.

For example: If you post something on your Facebook Page, and five people share it to their own timelines, and then five people share it from each of those timelines....then your update appears on 25 timelines, exposing it to many hundreds or even thousands of people who would not have seen it otherwise.

If you have really fascinating content, then you might be able to pull this off simply by doing your updates. However, sometimes it is hard to get people to share your updates, even if they know who you are. So often what you have to do is basically bribe people to share your stuff.

An easy way to bribe someone is with a simple contest. Post an image and description of the prize, and make the rules that you just have to like and share the post to enter. When the contest is over, just pick a winner at random. Ask the winner to also post a picture on their account with the prize.

Liking and sharing is such an easy way to enter a contest that many people will do it just because they have a chance to win something without doing a lot of work. And their odds are good.

Bribery works.

Facebook Advertising

Facebook advertising can be very effective and much less costly than using something like Google AdWords. However, unlike Google, who are masters at reaching into your pocket to get your money, Facebook tends to make things way harder than they need to be.

The easiest way to start advertising on Facebook is by boosting your posts. What this means is that you pay money to have your update appear to other Facebook users, whether they follow your Page or not. When you boost the post, you should select an audience that is targeted toward the subject of the post. To perform a boost, just click the Boost Post button beneath the post.

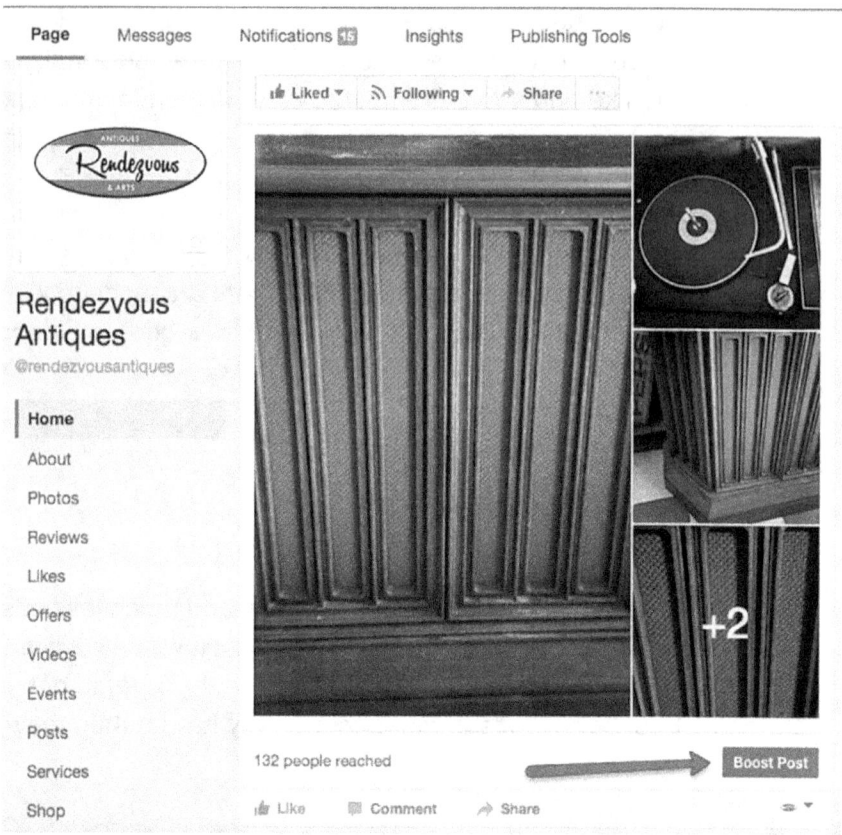

Facebook has some nice targeting options, including sex, age range, location, and interests. Facebook seems to do a pretty good job of matching your targeting to the correct prospects.

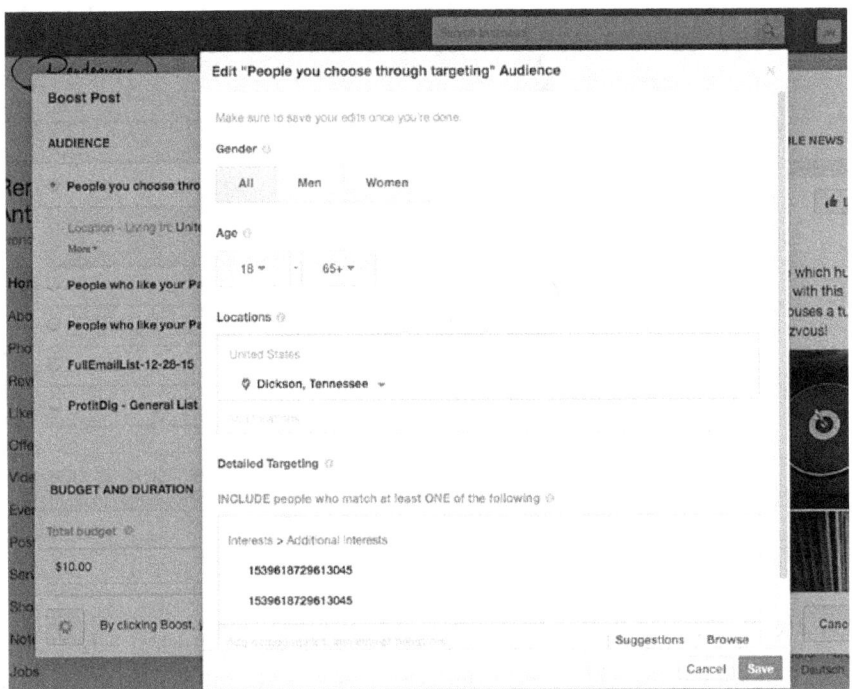

Facebook will show you how many impressions, clicks and such you got from paid boosted impressions versus organic impressions. Especially early on, you will probably find that you get many, many more impressions from your boosted updates.

Boosting your posts is not the only way to advertise on Facebook. Another option is to just create a standalone ad promoting your Page or business. To do that, go to your Ads Manager page (which you can access from the main menu on the left-hand side of the screen of the main Facebook page), and then click the Create Ad button.

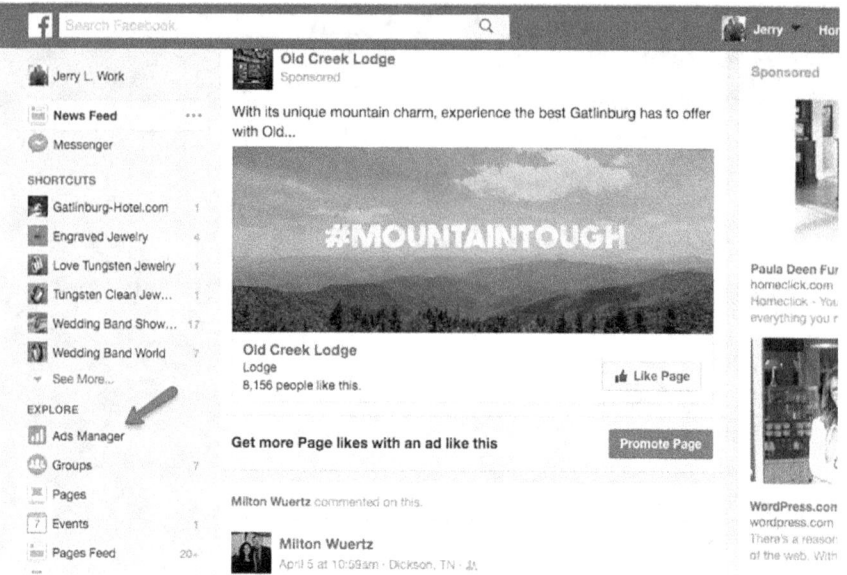

At this point, the process becomes similar to running ads on Google. You will name your campaign, set your targeting, set your daily budget, write the ad copy, etc. One thing about Facebook that I have never liked is that it is not as transparent as Google with regards to how much you should expect to pay per click. I will say, however, it will likely be less per click (or engagement) than you would pay in Google.

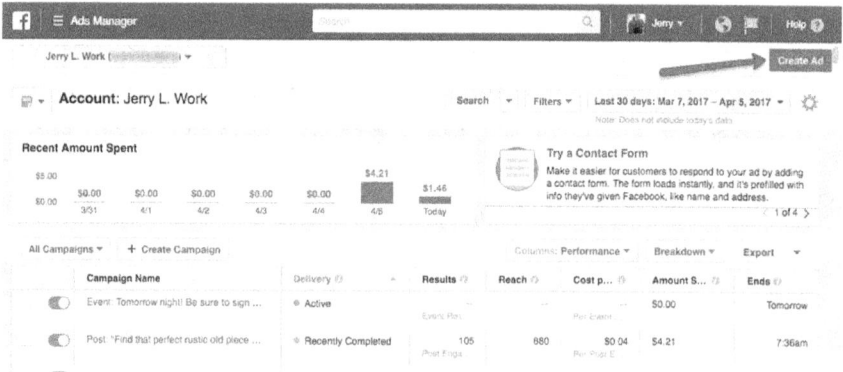

Likes on your Facebook page are certainly not the same thing as someone actually giving you money. But what you're doing is building name recognition among your target market and presenting them with targeted marketing messages. All of this stuff just serves to put people in the pipeline (your sales funnel). Then you still have to persuade those people to be your customer.

A word of caution: In my experience, Facebook marketing works well within the Facebook system and is probably reasonably accurate as far as reported clicks and such. But I have found that Facebook stats don't even come close to matching up with website analytics. So I am not sold on the effectiveness of Facebook to drive traffic to a website any cheaper than using Google AdWords or other platforms. So if you do use Facebook to drive website traffic, check your website analytics carefully to make sure you are actually getting traffic.

Videos are great content for Facebook updates as well. If you can show some real personality or make them very funny, people might share them. But I would also boost them as well.

Try to get 1,000 likes for your Page. Then keep going. You won't get to a thousand without working your account.

Facebook recently released something called Business Manager, which is a way to manage multiple Facebook advertising accounts from a single login. Great idea, but it's not the easiest thing to use. My advice is to avoid Business Manager unless you manage multiple Pages for other people. Otherwise, you will just be making things complicated for yourself.

Most of my social media discussion here has focused on Facebook because it is the platform that I think is most important for hotels and other lodging businesses. It still allows you the highest degree of interaction with potential clients and is the one most likely used by your potential customers.

YouTube and Videos

Videos should be used for social media updates, as discussed earlier, as well as added to your YouTube channel.

To set up a YouTube channel, first log into your Google account, then go to https://www.youtube.com and click the Sign in button. Then just follow the instructions. What you are going to do is set up your own "channel" - which is like your own little Internet TV channel.

Optimize your videos for specific keywords. Use the keywords in your video titles and descriptions. When uploading a video to YouTube, look at the description more like a complete webpage than just a brief description. Google loves video. There have been times in my work when I was able to get a YouTube video ranked very highly for high competition keywords.

YouTube also has its own video advertising system that can work very well for generating views of your videos to target audiences at a very low cost.

After posting a video to YouTube, use it for social media updates, website updates, etc.

Email

By now, email may seem like sort of an old fashion way of doing things. But the fact is it still works if you do it correctly. What you want to do is build your own email list of people who know who you are (preferably having stayed at your hotel) and who voluntarily agreed to receive your messages.

Having your own list of people who have volunteered to receive messages from you is a powerful position to be in from a marketing standpoint. And it is okay for you to put your visitors' email addresses into an email marketing list. Since they have conducted business with you, that is not considered spam. However, you must remove anyone who requests to be removed from your list.

It is a fantastic idea to have an email signup form on your website. Make it prominent. If someone really likes your hotel or your website and is willing to voluntarily receive email messages from you, then you should make it REALLY easy to do so. That signup form can also serve as the conversion event you use to measure performance from other marketing channels such as paid search.

One thing to keep in mind is that people have short memories. Once they sign up, you should begin to send emails quickly and regularly. Some of this can be automated. You can use a tool called an autoresponder to send a pre-programmed series of email messages to new subscribers.

Emailing your customers regularly also gives you a better chance at rebooking those same guests. It is common knowledge in marketing that it is always much cheaper to sell something to an existing customer than to get a new customer.

As you build up your email list, you are going to need to send out emails on a regular basis, and it can't all be automated. It is a good idea to send email newsletters that are not just promotional in nature but that also provide useful information to the reader. People are much less likely to unsubscribe from your list if you provide them value.

The same stuff you write about for your website and social media updates can be used for your newsletter content – local events, restaurant reviews, that kind of thing. Combine that kind of information with promotional offers and you have a winning formula.

Also take advantage of your email list to send seasonal messages. You should have a good idea if there are particular times of the year when people book more rooms. Take advantage of that information by using your email list to do promotional messages during those times, as well as promotions during off-peak times to try to fill empty rooms. Be strategic.

Email Marketing Companies

You will need to sign up with an email list company. Here are a few that are popular:

- www.constantcontact.com
- www.mailchimp.com
- www.sendgrid.com
- www.verticalresponse.com
- www.myemma.com

There are probably many more, but the above listed companies are all very reputable and have been in business a long time. I honestly can't recommend any one. I am currently using mostly Mailchimp. But any of the above companies will work just fine.

Email Signup Form

Your email list company will provide you with the code you need to use on your website to allow visitors to sign up. What will happen is that when the signup form is submitted, the information will be submitted to the email server to add to your list. What you want to happen after that is for the email company server to redirect the visitor to a thank you / confirmation page.

That thank you page is where your paid search conversion script will reside, if you are running ads. So if you are using paid search, every time a paid visitor arrives at your website and signs up for your list, you know what ad and keyword resulted in the conversion.

In Google Analytics, you would set the thank you page as a goal. Every time someone submitted the form and arrived at that page, it would be reported in analytics as a conversion. This will tell you how many conversions happened from organic search, paid search, social media, email, or anything else.

One thing Google Analytics won't show you is exactly what organic Google search queries were used. It's a whole security-related thing I won't go into. But you can pretty much find out everything else from Google Analytics.

As far as the design and layout of the email you send out, your email list provider will likely have templates you can use that will give the email a very professional look. Just select a template, add your content and images, and the email should look very professional.

When doing an email broadcast, I highly advise that you send a test email to yourself first to make sure that everything looks correct.

Analytics

Analytics is performance information about your website. It means things like:

- How many people have visited your website.

- Where those people came from.

- How long they stayed on your website.

- What pages they visited.

I shouldn't have to tell you, but I will anyway: it is very important to know how your website is performing. Analytics will also help you figure out your return on investment - how many dollars you are making for every dollar you spend on your marketing.

There are different options for analytics, but these days most businesses use Google Analytics. Here is what to do:

- Visit www.google.com/analytics and follow the instructions to log in or create a Google account if you don't have one.

- Once you are signed into a Google Analytics account, get the Google analytics script by clicking the admin icon (that looks like a gear) on the main menu.

- Look for the link that says "Tracking Info." Click that, then click the link that says "Tracking Code."

- Copy and paste the code that it presents to you on every page of your website, or in a footer file that is included on every page.

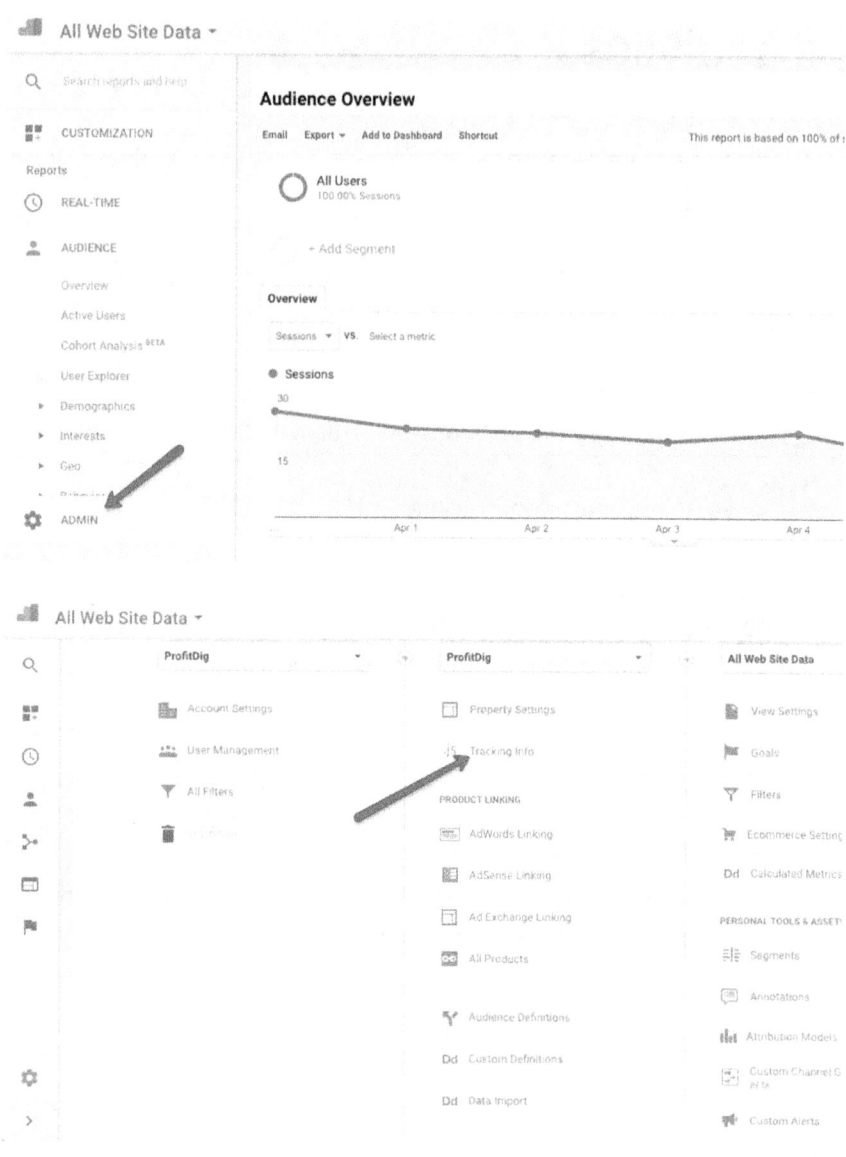

That is a super quick description of how this process works as of this writing, but Google changes this stuff up all the time. The main point is to find the Google analytics code, wherever it is, and paste it into every page of your site. Most likely, you will only have to paste it into a single footer file, which will update all of the pages automatically.

Analytics can be a complicated topic, so I'm not going to take up a whole lot of time talking about it here. But don't skip this step. Getting analytics installed on your website is the first and most important step in gauging the performance of your Internet marketing.

Conversion Tracking

In marketing, it is very important to remember that the whole point of all of it is to generate conversions. A conversion is the accomplishment of a specific goal. In its most basic form, a conversion is when someone gives you money. If someone clicks on an ad in Google, arrives at your website and then books a room – that is a conversion. The kinds of conversions you are most concerned with are this type of monetary transaction. But there are other types of conversions.

Maybe your conversion goal for a particular marketing campaign is to get people to sign up for your mailing list. In that case, a conversion would happen when someone signs up for your mailing list. After someone submits the form to sign up for your mailing list, he is redirected to a "thank you" page.

That thank you page should only load in someone's browser after submitting the form. So if submission of the signup form is considered a conversion, then you would set the URL of the thank you page as a goal. Once you do this, analytics will tell you all kinds of things about the people who sign up for your list.

To get monetary conversion tracking working correctly, you will have to figure out how to integrate it with your booking system. Somehow your booking engine has to pass the details of the transaction to a conversion tracking script.

If you use Google AdWords or another advertising platform, you will likely have a separate conversion tracking script to use. Google has a service called Tag Manager that can make it easier to manage multiple tracking scripts. To learn more about that, visit www.google.com/analytics/tag-manager.

Conversion Rate

Conversion rate is the percentage of people who have been exposed to your marketing who convert.

So if you run an ad on Google, and it gets 500 clicks, and 5 of those visitors convert, then your conversion rate is 1% (5 / 500).

In Internet marketing, cost per acquisition, as discussed above, is usually called cost per conversion.

Conclusion

Look y'all, I left out a mountain of details here. This book could easily be 5X longer if I REALLY went into specifics. But this is meant to be a somewhat high level overview of the things you need to do to promote your property online, with enough detail to get you going.

Is this stuff easy? Not really. But it ain't rocket science either. The main thing is giving yourself the time to do it. If you can't find the time, then hire someone to do it for you. If you do seek outside help, the knowledge in this book will make sure that you understand what your Internet marketing guy is doing. You will be much less likely to be fooled.

I do invite you to contact my company, Work Media, if you don't know where to turn. We would be proud to talk to you about how we can help your hotel or other lodging business. You can call us at 615-375-8793, email us at info@workmedia.net, or visit us online at www.workmedia.net.

Good luck!